Redlands REMEMBERED

Stories from the Jewel of the Inland Empire

Joan Hedges McCall

THE History PRESS

Published by The History Press
Charleston, SC 29403
www.historypress.net

Back cover images of modern orange grove and the Morey House courtesy of Caroline McAllister. Others courtesy of the A.K. Smiley Public Library.

All images are courtesy of the A.K. Smiley Public Library unless otherwise noted.

First published 2012

Manufactured in the United States

ISBN 978.1.60949.618.0

Library of Congress CIP data applied for.

Notice: The information in this book is true and complete to the best of our knowledge. It is offered without guarantee on the part of the author or The History Press. The author and The History Press disclaim all liability in connection with the use of this book.

Contents

Contents

Preface

Like a good novel, the nonfiction stories of the past should touch us in the present. We need facts, of course, and the lists of dates, places and begats give context, but none of it matters without the who-did-what-and-where. The facts mean nothing if we cannot connect them to our lives or circumstances or to the current events around us. Clothing, hair and furniture styles change the way things look. Technology changes the way we accomplish our daily tasks. Yet underneath it all, we humans behave in human ways. The stories of Redlands, of the people who have made this place their home, never fail to intrigue. As they transformed the local environment from dry chaparral to Victorian jewel, the people of Redlands brought an energy, inventiveness and civic dedication that continues today.

I grew up in a small but historically interesting town in Missouri. The early years of my marriage were spent in Philadelphia, steeped in the stories of America's beginning years. By the time we moved to Redlands, California, I was primed to embrace the interesting history of the area, as well as the town in particular. I signed up for the Redlands history course taught by Larry Burgess, then the archivist for the A.K. Smiley Public Library, and Tom Atchley, a popular history teacher at Redlands High School. I read numerous articles by both of these gentlemen and others and began my own history with the town. Some years later, looking for a way to reinvent myself as my children were ready to leave the nest, I began writing a monthly column, "Regarding Redlands," for the *Redlands Daily Facts*.

At first, I was content to retell the stories already told by those who came before me: Edith Parker Hinckley; Professor Lawrence E. Nelson; *Redlands Daily Facts* publisher William G. Moore and his brother, *Facts* editor Frank E. Moore; A.K. Smiley Public Library director Larry Burgess; historian Tom Atchley; and others. Then I discovered the bound newspapers in the Heritage Room at the A.K. Smiley Public Library. I remember furiously taking notes from one of these volumes one day when Frank Moore walked by. Frank stopped to say hi and told me that it was good to see me doing original research. That was the moment I began to view myself as a history storyteller in my own right.

The stories in this book represent some of the retellings and original research I have done for columns and feature articles for the *Facts*. I did not set out to chronicle the history of the town of Redlands, only to tell stories, with my personal observations, that have made it a unique place. Each part is a loose category, not a chronological time period. The anecdotes range from the early years of the Californios to more modern times. This is not an attempt to produce an academic text of the history of Redlands, and any errors are fully on my shoulders. I hope my readers will enjoy these human accounts that illustrate the way Redlands came to be the "Jewel of the Inland Empire."

Acknowledgements

Thanks are due to the people who have helped make this book a reality: Rhea-Frances Tetley for pushing me to propose my idea to the folks at The History Press; Nelda Stuck for taking the time to go through my manuscript with her trained and careful eye, making suggestions of form and substance; friends Kristina Naftzter and Donna Zdrojewski for their suggestions for updates and additions; and walking buddies Barbara Marcum and Danielle Wuchenich for their willingness to be early-morning sounding boards and last-minute proofreaders. Thank you to Caroline McAllister for her beautiful photographs and great sense of humor.

For forty years, the folks at the A.K. Smiley Public Library, especially in the Heritage Room, have provided an amazing resource for researchers and history buffs. Archivist Don McCue is always helpful. Assistant Archivist Nathan Gonzales has patiently let me pester him in person and via e-mail. Library Director Larry Burgess introduced me to the fascinating history of our town thirty years ago, encouraged me to "go for it" when I came asking for advice about writing a newspaper column and offered kind words when I decided to turn my columns and articles into this book.

I've appreciated my commissioning editor, Jerry Roberts, for giving me positive encouragement and prompt replies.

Special thanks go to my husband, Allan, for being the best.

Part I
Before Redlands Blossomed

If those with an interest to develop the as-yet-untouched areas of the San Bernardino Valley think that things are difficult these days, they should have been here in the early to mid-1800s. The Franciscan padres from San Gabriel Mission were the first nonnatives to recognize the potential of the Redlands area. A priest recorded: "In the year 1819, at the request of the unchristianized Indians of the place they call Guachama ["Place of Plenty to Eat"]...we began the introduction of cattle raising and farming...The place has an abundance of water...There is enough for irrigation."

"Enough for irrigation." Those were the magic words that would eventually turn the dry chaparral into a fertile garden, but it wasn't going to be easy.

It is not clear that the "unchristianized Indians of the place they call Guachama" actually made a request for the European settlers to invade the valley. The San Bernardino Valley is the place where the traditional cultural territories of the Serranos (fanning northwest through the mountains and over the Cajon Pass on to the high desert) and Cahuillas (spreading southwest through the mountains and over the San Gorgonio pass to the low desert) came together. For centuries, the tribes of these two cultural groups lived in permanent villages scattered throughout the area. These two groups of people lived off the land; their staples included the piñon nuts from the pine trees and a dish made from the acorns of the oak trees. Like other native people, the local tribes were forced onto reservations in the late 1800s and suffered greatly as the trickle of outsiders turned into a flood that claimed their historical lands and pushed them out of their homes.

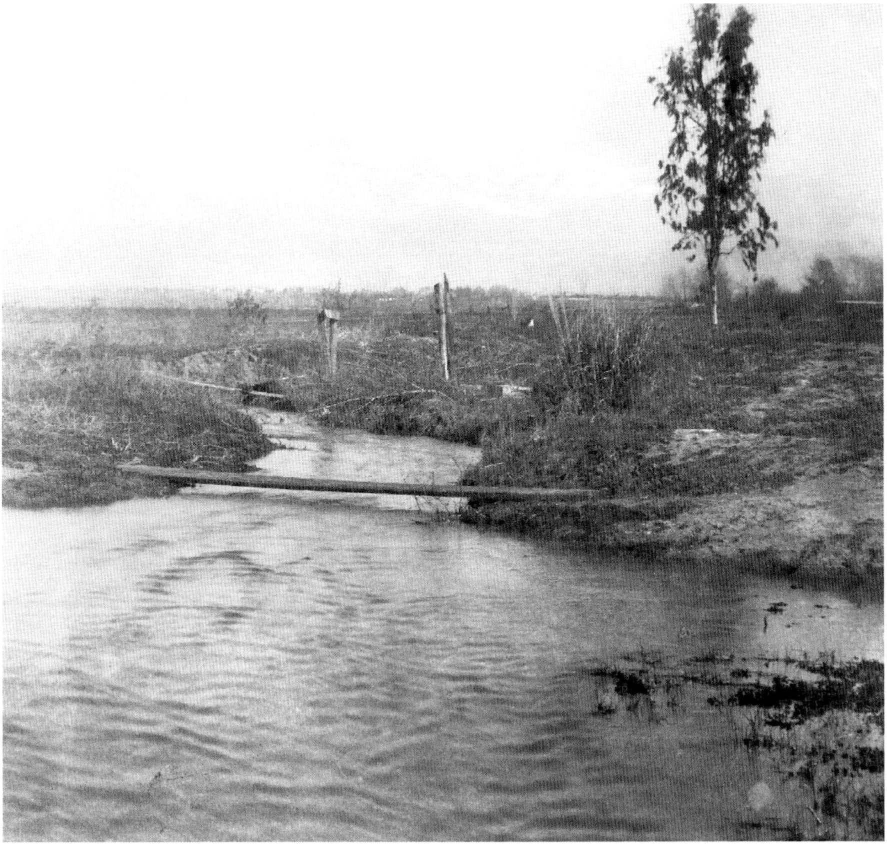

Priests from the San Gabriel Mission sought to bring water from Mill Creek to a naturally fertile area at the mouth of San Timoteo Canyon. Local natives dug the Mill Creek Zanja by hand in 1812. It starts at the eastern end of Mentone, meanders through Redlands and was designed to serve an estancia, or outpost to support cattle grazing. The buildings on Barton Road, today known as the Asistencia, are actually reproductions built in the 1930s. The original estancia was located about one mile to the east.

By 1820, the padres had enlisted the local natives and finished the first irrigation project in the valley. The ten-mile-long Mill Creek Zanja, or "Sankey," was dug by hand using shovels fashioned from available implements such as rocks and the shoulder blades of oxen. Understandably, many of the local tribes were not particularly happy with the European interlopers, and the remote location was difficult for the padres to defend. By 1834, the San Gabriel priests had given up.

Between the 1830s and 1880s, large landowners of Spanish and Mexican descent, called Californios, built ranches up and down California. Over this period, California was claimed by Spain, then Mexico and, finally, the United States. California became a state in 1850.

In 1839, Don Antonio Maria Lugo, a prominent Californio from Los Angeles, received permission to establish a ranch and colony in the San Bernardino Valley. The Lugos' growing numbers of cattle and horses needed expanded grazing lands, and the fertile plains at the mouth of the Santa Ana River seemed perfect. While we honor the Lugos with the name Lugonia, they didn't stay.

Plentiful water and easy transportation were two keys to the development of much of Southern California. Few recall that the San Bernardino Valley owes some of both to one of the Lugo colonists, a woman by the name of Maria Armenta Bermudez. Maria Armenta married Jose Bermudez in 1823. Jose was thirty years older than Maria, and they both probably worked for the Lugo family. Jose first built a house in the area where the San Bernardino Courthouse now stands. One of the Lugo sons moved into that house, and the Bermudez family settled across the valley in what is now Redlands.

Maria wanted to grow grapes, but the closest water supply was the Zanja, about two miles away. Maria arranged for a ditch to be dug from the Zanja to her property near what is now Ford Park. She laid out the channel, beginning near the current site of Crafton Elementary School, following along the base of the hills. Known as the Maria Armenta Ditch (the only zanja to be named after a woman), the route was so well designed that, years later, the Bear Valley Water District followed it when it built its canal to the original Ford Park reservoir. The remains of Maria's vineyards were visible testimony to the future prospects of the area when Americans Edward Judson and Frank Brown bought Redlands property more than thirty years later.

The Bermudez family moved on and settled in San Timoteo Canyon, first near the mouth of Live Oak Canyon and finally down on the south side of what is now Barton Road, near the area called Guachama. Here, Maria planted large fields of grain and corn and carried her produce to market in Los Angeles in two-wheeled carretas drawn by oxen. The remote San Bernardino area was connected to Los Angeles by a mere footpath until Maria enlarged it into a full-sized road for her ox carts. The sixty-mile trip must have taken three to four days each way.

In 1847, government records show that Maria applied for a parcel of land "on the other side of the Los Angeles River." Maria's stated reason for the application was her need to earn a livelihood for her family. After such a long journey, her oxen needed a rest stop in Los Angeles. Her petition was granted. Jose was by now seventy-nine years old and unfit for strenuous labor. Although he had fathered their nine children along the way, Maria was definitely the one responsible for her family.

Maria Armenta Bermudez was a true pioneer. It is hard to believe that anyone could survive the birth of nine children in a time of frequent Indian and outlaw attacks, all the while running a thriving truck farm. She stayed in the valley long after others came and gave up. It is sad to note that she died of tetanus said to have been contracted by stepping on a sharp stick as she jumped a ditch on her farm. This was clearly a woman of vision and fortitude.

The next time you are tempted to complain about the traffic jam at Kellogg Hill on the commute between Redlands and Los Angeles, remember Maria Bermudez and her ox carts.

HANNAH SMITH EMBERS, A LOCAL PIONEER

Martha Embers Beal, wife of pioneer Redlander Israel Beal, carried a remarkable legacy. In 1856, when Martha was two years old, her mother, Hannah Smith Embers, along with fellow slave Biddy Smith Mason, sued their master for their freedom. The story of their bravery has been told by several historians, including Clyde A. Milner II writing in *The Oxford History of the American West*. This is their story.

Much of the history of the West is a story of journeys. Hannah and Biddy, two African American women, followed an ox cart all the way to the San Bernardino Valley from Georgia. In the beginning, they had no choice in the matter. They were slaves of Robert Smith, a Mormon convert. Fortitude, fortune and the help of a friend gained them their freedom.

In 1844, Smith and his family joined a group known as the Mississippi Company as it traveled west to join other Mormons, heading eventually for Utah. While the Mormon Church did not sanction slavery, some members of the party kept their slaves anyway.

Another family in the Mississippi Company was that of Bishop William Crosby and his slaves, two of whom were brothers, Grief and Toby Embers. Toby would become Hannah's husband. Also in the group was the Flake family, including their slave, Elizabeth, known as Lizzie. Lizzie married Charles Rowan in San Bernardino, and they became quite prosperous in later years.

The Smith, Crosby and Flake families became part of the Amasa M. Lyman and Charles C. Rich party of about five hundred people, including twenty-six African Americans, who moved on west in 1851 to settle the San Bernardino Valley. The trek from Salt Lake was arduous. Fear of attack by hostile Indians and outlaws competed with the monotony of the trail. The trip took three months.

It is hard to imagine the conditions of this westward migration. Each family loaded one wagon with their belongings. Room to ride in the wagon would have been limited, so most made the trip on foot. The few accounts from descendants of the slaves tell us that these women walked, driving the livestock while taking care of the master's children as well as their own.

Lyman and Rich negotiated the purchase of the Lugo Rancho from the Lugo family, who were giving up because of the dangers associated with its remote location.

It was the summer of 1851, and the only man-made landmarks in the valley were the Mill Creek Zanja, dug by local Indians for the Spanish padres thirty years earlier, a few dwellings and barns constructed by the Lugos, and some Serrano and Cajuilla villages. The new settlers were very well organized. Their first task was the construction of a stockade. Each family was responsible for a certain length of the wall, and once complete, they built small homes for themselves inside the fort. Wheat fields were planted, and roads were developed into the mountains to retrieve the lumber.

Grief Embers achieved a place in the history books because he had a six-foot horn, which he used to call the settlers to work in the fields and to alert them to danger.

As the fear of marauders lessened, the streets of San Bernardino were laid out, and homes were built outside the fort. In September 1852, the colony held a Harvest Feast. The *Los Angeles Star* reported, "In this miniature World's Fair, several hundred people of both sexes assembled at 10 A.M. in their best dress, forming a beautiful representation of an American assembly of every

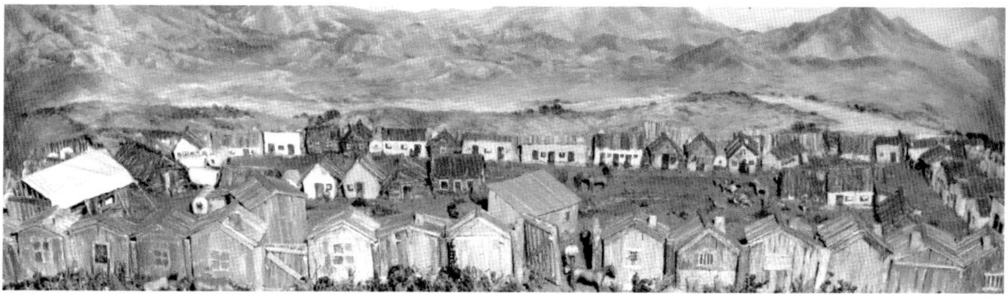

This model of Fort San Bernardino shows how the homes were put together to form a combined stockade and village.

age and condition; and this bright picture shaded in the background with a few specimens of representatives of the Spanish, Indian, and African races."

California had joined the Union as a free state in 1850. Rumors may have reached the slaves in San Bernardino concerning their new legal status, but white owners suppressed the information that they were automatically free once they crossed the state line. Martha Beal said in later years that her people had originally been afraid to live without the protection of their owners but easily made the adjustment.

By 1855, the settlement of San Bernardino had turned into a full-fledged town. The county of San Bernardino had been formed (it included what we now know as the county of Riverside), and the area was under the legal jurisdiction of a circuit judge by the name of Benjamin Hayes.

Hayes's diaries show that he was well known throughout his district and that he had an interest in the downtrodden. There were so few African Americans living in San Bernardino that it is possible he met Hannah and Biddy soon after their arrival.

In 1856, Robert Smith decided to take his family (and his slaves) to Texas, which was still a slave state. There are no diaries or oral legends to tell us Hannah and Biddy's reactions when they heard this news. Biddy, age thirty-eight, had three daughters, aged eight to seventeen. Hannah's life was more complicated. She was thirty-four years old and had eight children, from newborn to seventeen years old, and one grandchild, aged two. No mention is made of Hannah's husband, Toby Embers, but presumably, he was to stay behind with the Crosby family.

We know that Hannah was the midwife to the San Bernardino colony. She was an expert horsewoman and was said to be cheerfully available, at any hour, to perform her tasks. She must have been strong and intelligent, though uneducated, and it is easy to speculate that she, Biddy and Lizzie Rowan cooked up the plot that resulted in their freedom.

Robert Smith packed up his family, including Biddy and Hannah and their children. Biddy's daughter takes up the tale:

> [T]*he master decided to take the slaves and his family to Texas. En route, they journeyed through Los Angeles County, and camped in a canyon near Santa Monica, where they had spent only a few days when the news reached Los Angeles, through a Mrs. Rowan, of San Bernardino, that these slaves were leaving California to go back into slavery in Texas. The Sheriff of Los Angeles County…issued a writ against this slave-master, preventing him from taking his slaves from the State of California.*

Why didn't Biddy and Hannah simply refuse to go with Smith? They were bound by a lifetime of obedience, for one. In addition, rumors of runaway slaves being chased and returned to their masters competed with their limited understanding of the laws of the state. Maybe if they had been able to go before the judge, he could give them the official papers that would have declared them free. They had everything to lose and everything to gain.

The group was brought before Judge Hayes on January 19, 1856. Hayes ruled that the two women and their children were being forcibly removed from California, declared them all free and ordered Smith to pay their travel expenses and court costs.

Biddy Mason and her children moved to Los Angeles. She worked as a nurse, saved her money and began buying property. She became a leader in the African American community and helped many struggling newcomers to that city. Hannah went home to Toby.

The majority of the Mormon colony was soon called back to Utah, but the former slaves remained in Southern California. Grief Embers became one of the first African American property owners in San Bernardino. Lizzie and Charles Rowan raised a daughter, who was the first African American woman to graduate from the Los Angeles Normal School. She became a teacher in Riverside. Little Martha Embers grew up to marry Israel Beal of Redlands. Their sons, Arthur and Harry, would be among the earliest athletes and graduates of Redlands High School.

The shared journeys of these families laid the foundation for the ties that remain today between the African American communities of Redlands, San Bernardino and Riverside.

The Suburbs of Redlands Came Before the City Itself

Lying many hundred feet above the level of the sea, Lugonia has a surpassingly charming climate, not excelled in the State, and the light winds from the ocean blow constantly through the summer.

—*Wallace Elliot*, History of San Bernardino County, *1883*

It is an amazing thing the way Redlands came to pass. The suburbs grew before the town itself was established; there was a semi-circle of settlements around our location just as though the circumference of the wheel was built before the hub. These settlements were first, the Mission district around the

> *Asistencia; second, Crafon to the east; and third, Lugonia to the north. The key to the location of these settlements was water. For fifty years people hugged the zanja, that being the lifeline.*
>
> *–Edith Parker Hinckley,* On the Banks of the Zanja, *1951*

Newcomers to Redlands are often bemused by the territorial views and loyalties of the local inhabitants. North-siders suspect the south-siders of looking out only after themselves. Mentonites fear annexation attempts. Craftonites struggle to protect their rural quiet. Perhaps all of this distrust stems from the fact that Redlands developed last, but like a hub, it drives the wheel.

What happened in the thirty-seven-year period between the departure of the Lugos from San Bernardino Rancho and the incorporation of Redlands in 1888? The first American census in California was conducted in 1850. The San Bernardino Valley was surveyed by John R. Evertsen, who was paid two cents for each person listed and given an allowance of ten cents per mile for necessary travel.

I don't know if he ever got paid, because Evertsen's census document was lost until 1915 when, like a scene from one of his movies, early filmmaker Cecil B. DeMille happened to pass by a caretaker burning rubbish from an old adobe ranch house near Mission San Fernando. A package sticking out of the smoldering pile caught DeMille's eye. The package contained an old paper. Folded four times, this old paper was the record of the 1850 census of the San Bernardino Valley.

Evertsen counted fifty people living in the San Bernardino Valley in 1850: two Lugo households; the families of Francisco Aguella, Mariano Elisalda and Jose Bermudez; and the Indians who were employed as domestic servants. No count was made of Serranos or Cajuillas living apart from the settlers.

By 1851, the Lugos had become weary of life on the wild frontier. They had endured numerous attacks by wildlife (grizzly bear roping was a favorite pastime), outlaws and hostile Indians. They had watched helplessly as their cattle and horses were stolen or slaughtered by the hundreds. The Lugos took the opportunity to sell to a company of Mormons and moved back to civilization in Los Angeles.

Nearly five hundred stalwart Mormons trekked across the deserts and mountains from Salt Lake City in 1851. Their goal was the establishment of a Southern California colony that could act as a way station for new church members on their way to Salt Lake City from the ports of San Diego and Los Angeles. Once here, they purchased the more than thirty thousand acres of San Bernardino Rancho from the Lugo family for $77,500.

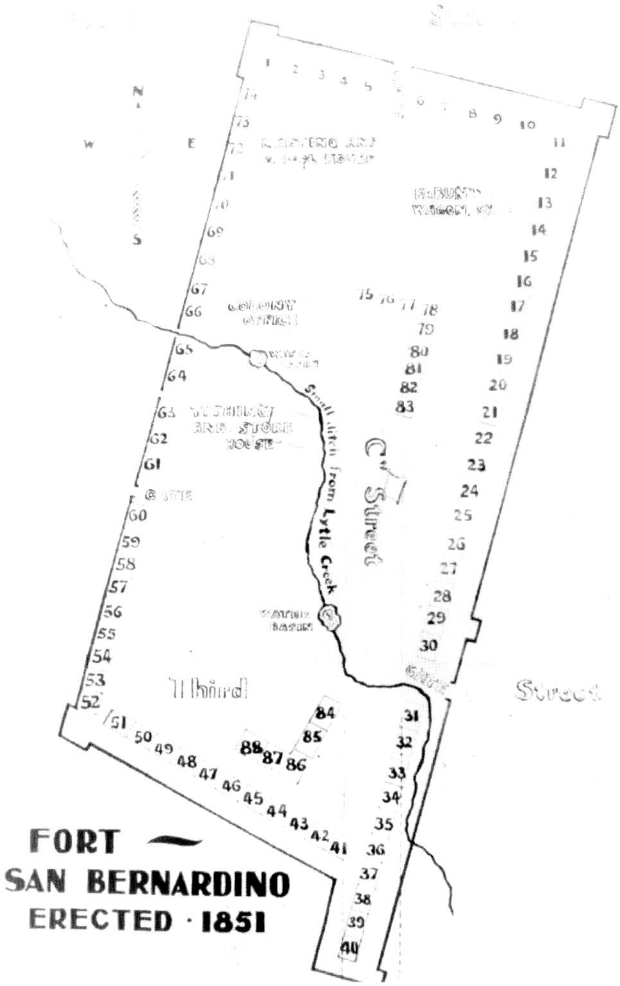

Map of Fort San Bernardino, showing its original location near the current county courthouse between today's Third and Fourth Streets in San Bernardino. A ditch brought water to the settlers from Lytle Creek.

The Mormons built a fort in San Bernardino, laid out vegetable and grain fields, built a road into the mountains for access to lumber and established stagecoach roads to Los Angeles and Salt Lake City. In a few short years, the town they built brought civilization and order to the San Bernardino Valley.

Once the town of San Bernardino was developed, the area around the Asistencia became known as Old San Bernardino. Bishop Nathan C. Tenney had charge of the agricultural work south of the Santa Ana River, and he and his family took up residence in the old Asistencia buildings. Mrs. Tenney started a school, and the bishop arranged for a new ditch to be dug to the area from the Santa Ana River, with the idea of supplementing the water in the Mill Creek Zanja (the original water ditch in this area was dug by local Indians at the behest of the Spanish padres in about 1820).

In one of the first of many water rights disputes, the residents of the north side of the Santa Ana River prevented Tenney from using his ditch. Later, it would be known as the Berry Roberts ditch and would play a part in the development of Lugonia.

The Mormons were unexpectedly called back to Salt Lake City in 1857. The valley went into a decline for several years. The once thriving town of San Bernardino, incorporated in 1854, was disincorporated in 1863. It was not until 1869 that things had stabilized enough for reincorporation.

For those left behind, the good news was that land was for sale at bargain prices. The most attractive location was Old San Bernardino. It would become known as the town of Mission, and its new chief landowner, Dr. Benjamin Barton, would provide a large part of the real estate, which would rise to greatness as the towns of Lugonia and Redlands.

Grapes Grew Before the Orange Boom

Dr. Benjamin Barton was a man in the right place at the right time.

The mostly Mormon settlement of San Bernardino was thrown into turmoil in 1857 when Brigham Young called his faithful to return to Salt Lake City. Six years of labor was to be abandoned and more than thirty thousand acres sold.

Barton and his wife, Eliza, had come to Southern California via the overland trail from El Paso, Texas, in 1854. They lived in El Monte for three years until word of opportunity in San Bernardino reached them. Along with several lots in the city of San Bernardino, Barton completed a major deal with Amasa Lyman and Charles Rich to purchase 640 acres in Mission (also called Old San Bernardino) for $5,000.

Barton established a pharmacy and medical practice in San Bernardino, but the town had changed after its founders' departure. As it struggled to find a new identity (it had lost two-thirds of its population and most of its leading citizens), San Bernardino became more of a frontier town. The accompanying lawlessness may have led the Bartons to look across the valley to their isolated Mission property.

In 1859, Dr. Barton moved his family into what remained of the adobe structure that we now call the Asistencia. Over the next twenty-seven years, Barton built a large brick villa just north of the Asistencia, landscaped the

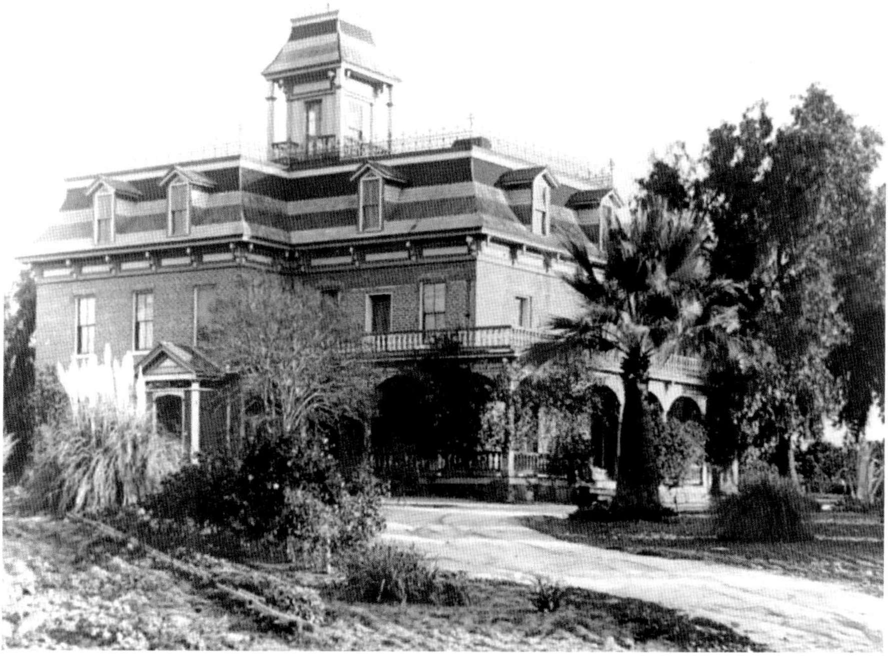

Dr. Benjamin Barton owned a large acreage on the south side of the Santa Ana River. His home was perched prominently on the crest of a hill near the old estancia and housed his medical office plus a schoolroom for the children of local settlers.

grounds with beautiful English gardens and lived the life of gentleman farmer. Barton continued to practice medicine from an office in his home. He built a schoolroom on the second floor and paid a teacher to conduct lessons for his children and those of his neighbors. At a time when most homes in the area were small, flat-roofed adobe structures, Barton's villa on top of its knoll must have seemed like a castle in the clouds.

The Barton Ranch eventually encompassed two to three thousand acres. Sheep grazed on the dry hills where Kingsbury School children play today. Barton vineyards, orchards and grazing land covered much of the area from Barton Road to what is now the University of Redlands. The vineyards produced grapes, which became popular delicacies in San Francisco and New York. They were packed in sawdust in sixty-pound boxes and shipped by coastal freighter. Barton's winery, named Brookside because of its location along the Zanja, produced thirty thousand gallons of wine in 1872. Eventually, Barton sold the winery to the Vache brothers, who continued to make wine under the Brookside label.

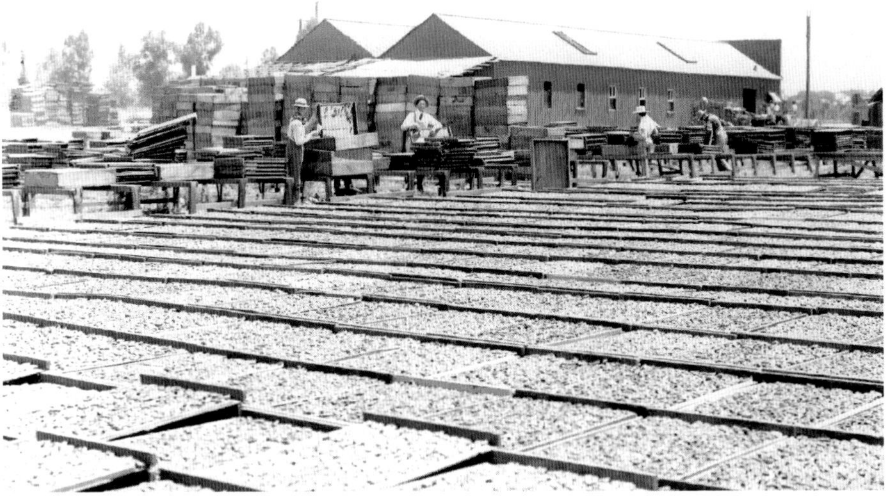

Before it was discovered that oranges fared well, many settlers grew the familiar fruits they knew in the East. This shows Arthur Gregory's apricot drying operation in about 1890.

Between 1881 and 1887, Barton began selling off his property, first to Edward Judson and Frank Brown and then to a consortium headed by his son, Hiram. His daughter, Mary, took charge of the Villa and its eighty-five acres. Ben and Eliza Barton moved to the now revitalized city of San Bernardino, built a large, modern home and retired from country life.

The Bartons were not the only landowners in Mission, of course. Some early family names were Curtis, Frink, Hinckley, Cole, Wilson, Pichon, Yount and Van Leuven.

Many varieties of fruit were grown in the valley, though none was dominant then. Apricots were profitable through World War I. Fruit dryers dotted the landscape years before the citrus packinghouses arrived. The Van Leuvens were the first to try growing oranges here. According to L.E. Nelson:

> *Anson Van Leaven of the Mission district reported: "I have eighty acres of land, planted mostly to oranges, peaches and apricot. Came here in 1853, and set out the first orange tree in this county…simply as an experiment. No one believed the climate to be adapted to their growth."*
>
> *He forgot to mention that he had not originated the idea, as his sister-in-law made clear in 1897: "In 1855, I visited Los Angeles and brought back and planted the seeds of an orange eaten there. Nearly all came up*

and four grew very well until about two years old, when my husband sold them to his brother Anson, who removed them to his own ranch, where they are still growing. After crying about it I resolved that no one should get the start of me in raising the first orange grove in this valley. I thereupon secretly dispatched Martin Chipman to Los Angeles with instructions to purchase fifty orange trees and return with them as soon as possible. My husband was informed in time to prepare the ground for their reception, and I was very glad to hear of his approval of my enterprise. In due time forty-five seedlings arrived and were set out on the old homestead, in 1857, where they are now flourishing."

The stage was set for the great land and citrus boom of the 1880s. Mission, with its established homes and orchards, looked to be the major township in the area.

However, Edward Judson and Frank Brown also happened to be in the right place at the right time. The town of Mission soon became a mere district swallowed by the newcomer, Redlands.

The Rain in Redlands Flows Mainly to the Sea

The Santa Ana River and the canyon it carves through our mountains have played major roles in shaping the San Bernardino Valley, as well as the lives of the towns in the river's path. Local Indians called the Santa Ana River the "upside-down river." A trip to the riverbed most times of the year usually makes you wonder, "What river?" Like the dusty hills near the coast that lure unsuspecting newcomers to build for the view, the dry riverbed is a disaster waiting for rain. Intermittent flash floods have been an example of the drama that can occur without warning. As the populations of the towns downstream from Redlands have grown, developers have been unable to resist the land that has historically been a flood plain for the Santa Ana. Why should flat and buildable land remain vacant? Flooding occurs infrequently enough that people forget, or choose to forget, the potential for disaster.

Frank E. Moore, in his book *Redlands: Our Town*, wrote:

There are high mountains—10,000 feet, and higher—east of Redlands. They wring the moisture out of our storms and it flows down into our valley in the Santa Ana River. This river flows down through Riverside and Orange counties to the sea at Newport Beach.

A series of agricultural communities were founded along the Santa Ana. Disappointed gold seekers established the first one, near the coast. They called it Anaheim. You probably know of it because Disneyland is there.

The climate proved to be excellent for oranges. The Santa Ana became the "string" on which "beads" were strung—Santa Ana, Orange, Corona, Riverside, Redlands.

The Mill Creek Zanja, known locally as the Sankey, was supplying water to the town of Lugonia in the 1880s when Frank Brown and Edward Judson surveyed the eastern end of the San Bernardino Valley and envisioned a new town in the hills supplied by water from the Santa Ana River.

Frank Brown's friend, Hiram Barton, son of Benjamin Barton, took Brown on a trek up the Santa Ana Canyon to a mountain area known as Bear Valley. Brown, a graduate of the Sheffield Scientific School at Yale University, took a look at the stream-fed mountain valley, which narrowed at its southern end before it dropped off to connect with the Santa Ana

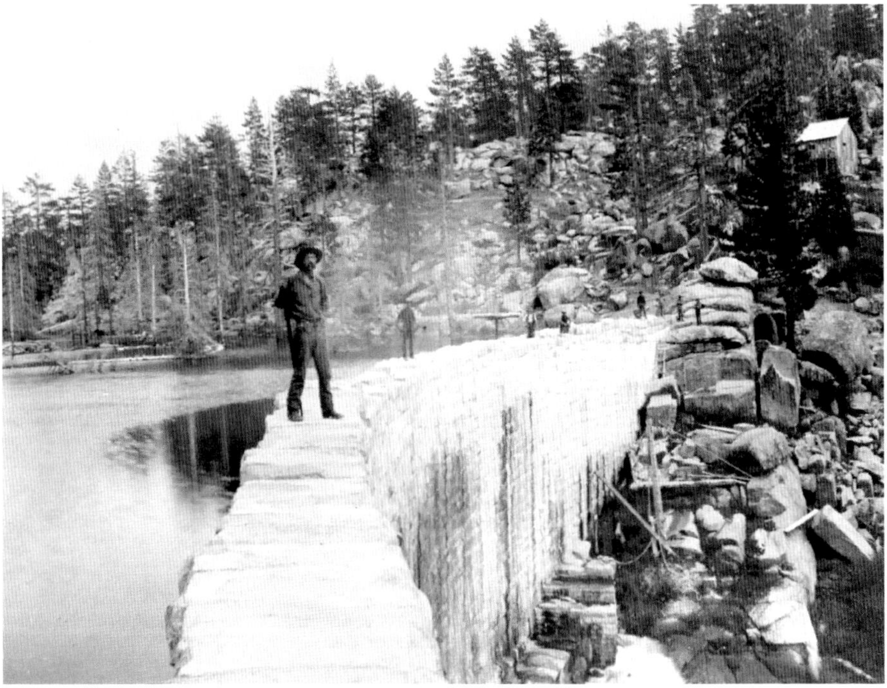

Frank Brown conceived this single-arch dam, completed in 1894, that turned Bear Valley into Big Bear Lake, a reservoir that supplied water to Redlands until late in the twentieth century.

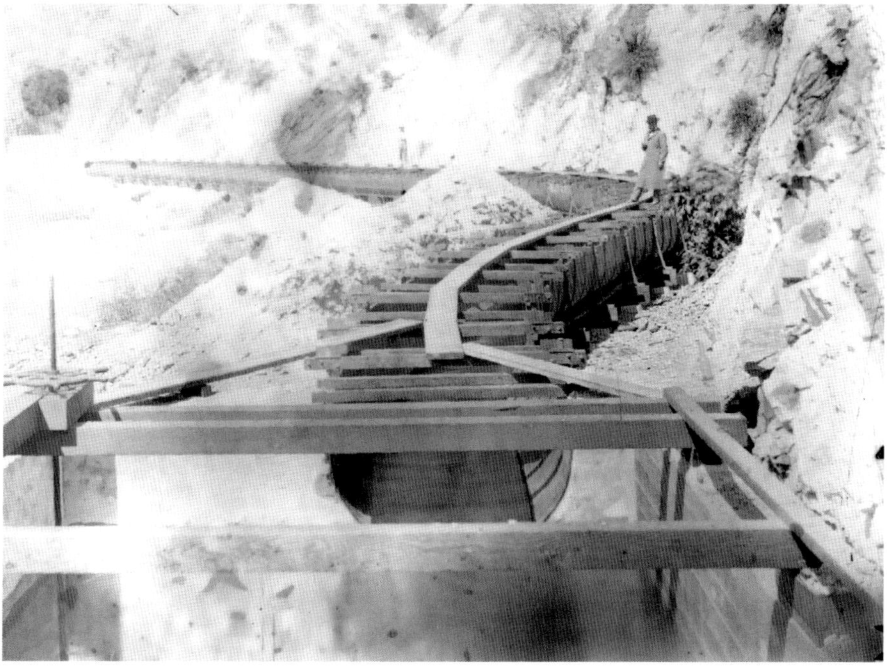

A wooden flume (open pipe) from Big Bear Lake carried the water through Santa Ana Canyon into a ditch running across the valley to a reservoir in the area now used as Ford Park. From there, gravity flow spread it out to the homes and businesses of the new town.

Canyon. His engineering marvel, a single arch dam, transformed Bear Valley from meadow to lake, and Big Bear Lake's pure mountain water became the source of health and happiness in the new town of Redlands. A wooden flume was built to carry water from Big Bear Lake, down the Santa Ana Canyon, to connect with the city's fledgling municipal waterworks.

Unfortunately, the water in the flume from Big Bear Lake is not the only water to flow down the Santa Ana Canyon. Normal annual runoff is fine, but a big rain turns the Santa Ana right side up, and too much of it spells trouble for towns along the river's path. Mrs. Eliza P.R. Crafts wrote of the winter of 1861–62:

> *The fall of 1861 was sunny, dry, and warm until Christmas, which proved to be a rainy day. All through the holidays there continued what we should call a nice, pleasant rain…This…lasted until the 18th of January, 1862, when there was a downpour for twenty-four hours, or longer… There were so many families rendered homeless that there was not a house*

in San Bernardino with only one family in it. Some sheltered three or more. The constant rain on the adobe houses turned them to mud, and of course they fell to pieces.

More than fifty inches of rain fell in 1861–62. Much of it came in that twenty-four-hour January downpour. A wall of water, described by witnesses as thirty-five to fifty feet high, roared down the Santa Ana, obliterated the town of Agua Mansa along its banks between Colton and Riverside and altered the course of the river.

The year 1867 saw another disastrous flood. Those living through both events said that there was more water in 1867. For two weeks in December, there were torrential rains. Fortunately, the deep channels cut five years earlier contained some of the damage, but again, farms and orchards along the river's course were destroyed.

The U.S. Army Corps of Engineers estimates that a recurrence of these flood conditions now would cause at least $15 billion in damage and flood much of Orange County. The Seven Oaks Dam, finished in 1999, was built for the purpose of holding back this type of once-in-a-hundred-years occurrence.

Still, rains in years since the dam's completion have washed out bridges and flooded homes as the water running down the mountainsides headed for the river. It is always a good idea to take to high ground whenever such an event turns the Santa Ana River right side up again.

Look to the Hills From Where Our History Comes

The San Bernardino Mountains rise from the northern edge of the valley and soar to heights topping eleven thousand feet above sea level. Originally home to two distinct ethnic groups, the Serranos and Cahuillas, the mountains were heavily forested with hemlock, cypress and pine. Water flows north from the range to form the headwaters of the Mojave River. Water flows to the south into the Santa Ana River and down to the Pacific Ocean. Redlands has always had a close relationship with Bear Valley, in the mountains to the northeast of town. Big Bear Lake there owes its existence to Redlands founders Frank Brown and Edward Judson, and our town owes its water security to the lake in return.

Lumbering operations in the San Bernardino Mountains go back to the Californio days. The canyon and stream we now call Mill Creek was the logical location for the first sawmill. The water ran dependably year round, and Louis Vignes, a well-known winemaker of the Aliso vineyard in Los Angeles, owned a mill in the lower reaches of Mill Creek Canyon. This mill, also known as the Aliso Mill and later the Chino Mill, supplied the wooden pipes that became the original water delivery system in Los Angeles. Mill Creek supplied the power for the mill operation and the water that drew ranchers and settlers along the valley floor alongside the Mill Creek Zanja.

The earliest American property owners in San Bernardino were the Mormons who jointly purchased the Lugo ranch in the 1850s. Once their stockade was built to protect them from marauding bandits and hostile natives, the Mormon colonists quickly realized that the best source of immediate income would be lumber sales to the burgeoning town of Los Angeles. Amasa Lyman and Charles Rich built a sawmill above the Vignes mill at a point where the big trees were available. This mill processed lumber from as far up as Forest Falls.

The big trees to the north, above the new town of San Bernardino, beckoned. The men of the Mormon colony determined that Waterman Canyon would provide the easiest access for the first road to the crest. They labored almost unceasingly until the road was completed. While most lumber roads were private toll roads, the Mormons' road was open to the public without a toll. This was not a trip for the faint of heart, though. In some areas, the grade was astoundingly steep, but it opened the mountains to the harvesting of trees. In the period between 1854 and 1856, the San Bernardino Mountains provided the lumber to build more than seven hundred buildings in the city of Los Angeles.

As time went on, most of the lumbering operations in the San Bernardino Mountains were portable affairs. The sawmill would be set up in the area to be cut and then moved to another location when the wood supply was depleted. One exception to this practice was the Brookings Mill. Originally called the Highland Lumber Company, the Brookings sawmill operation was located just below the current town of Running Springs. Narrow-gauge railroad tracks were laid in several directions. This way, they could clear-cut a section and bring the lumber back to the mill by train.

Getting the lumber from mill to market was another matter. Mules—and later, a narrow-gauge railroad—moved lumber to markets along the top of the mountain ridge. Horses moved the milled lumber down the mountain. An experienced teamster could bring his four-horse team and load from Brookings Mill to the Molino Box Factory in Highland in about three hours. The Highland Lumber Company built the original City Creek Road in 1891. Anyone else who wanted to use the roadway had to pay a toll and

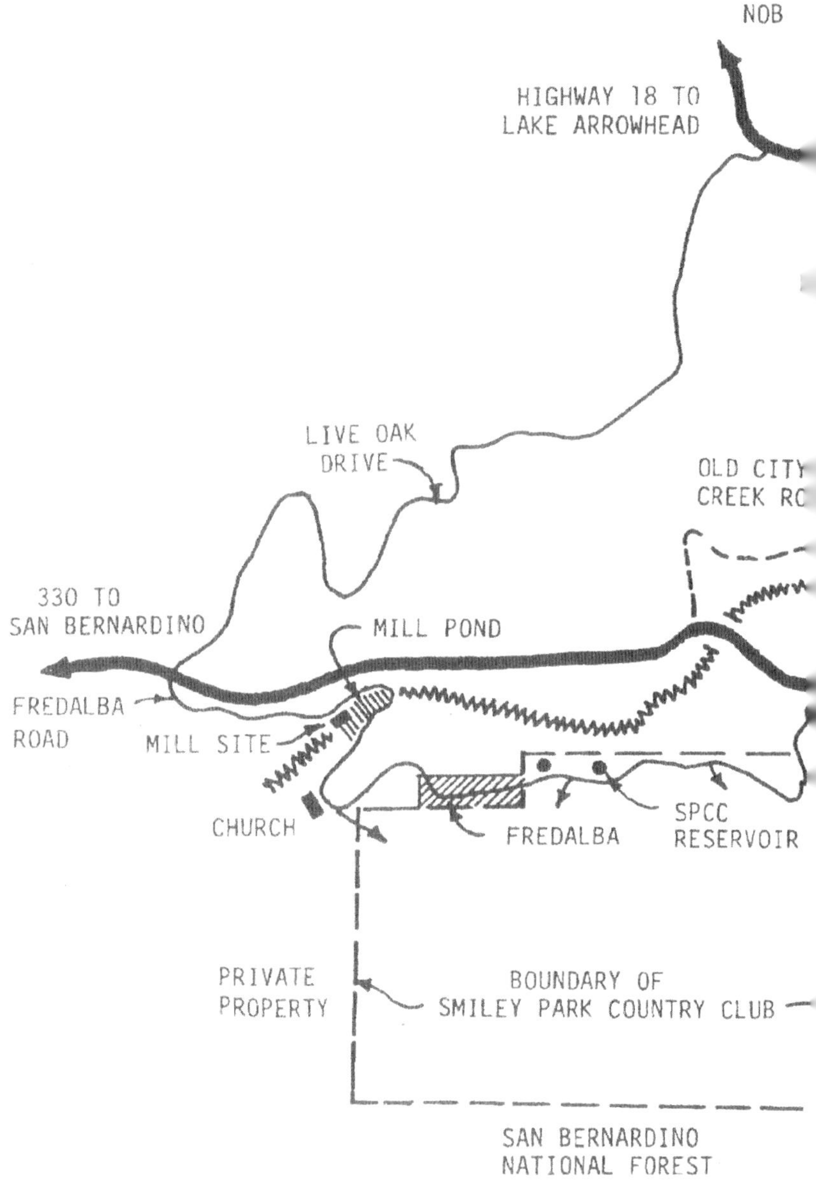

Area map of the San Bernardino Mounta

This map shows the location of the Brookings Mill, the Smiley Resort (called Fredalba) and the current residential area known as Smiley Park. *Courtesy Rhea-Frances Tetley.*

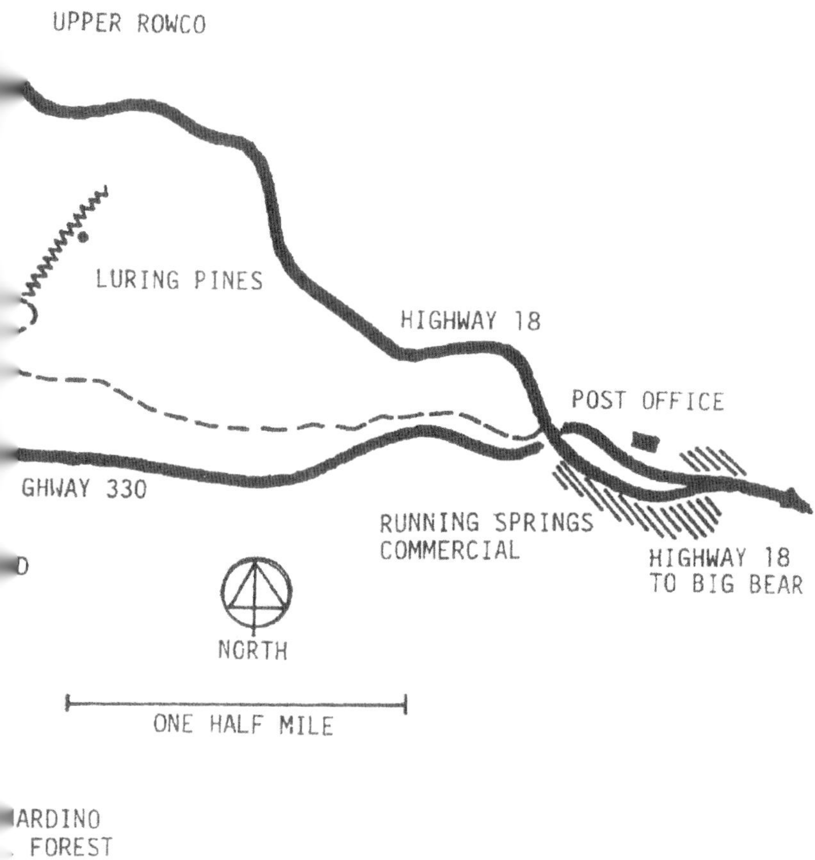

e location of Smiley Park and Fredalba

pray that they would not encounter one of those heavy, fast-moving lumber wagons at a point too narrow to pull out.

The Brookings Mill remained in operation until 1912, when a back-to-nature movement resulted in increased regulatory pressure. The San Bernardino National Forest was established in 1893, and the public began to regard the clear-cut lumbering methods with disfavor. The Brookings Mill was dismantled and its machinery shipped to Oregon. The logging railway was removed, and San Bernardino County took over the railroad right-of-way to construct the scenic Rim of the World Highway that runs along the top ridge of the eastern San Bernardino Mountains.

What was all that lumber used for? Besides homes and buildings from San Bernardino to Los Angeles, some of it went to build the boxes that shipped locally grown navel oranges to markets around the world.

The next time you take a holiday to enjoy one of our beautiful clear days, may I suggest a drive up the old City Creek Road (now Highway 330), through Running Springs, over the Rim of the World Drive and on to Arrowhead Village. If you choose the right day, you will be able to see Catalina Island in the distance.

Oh, and about those wooden water pipes? They leaked.

It's Easier to Get Here Now

To reach San Bernardino you take steamer at San Francisco for Los Angeles, which place you reach from San Pedro, its port, by a short railroad. The voyage, which lasts thirty-six hours, and is made all the way in sight of lands, is usually pleasant. From Los Angeles you get to San Bernardino by stage, distance sixty miles—time ten hours.

–California for Health, Pleasure, and Residence:
A Book for Travellers and Settlers, *Charles Nordhoff, 1873*

Charles Nordhoff made his first visit to California in the 1840s. Over the next thirty years, his love affair with the Golden State and its neighbor to the south—Lower, or Baja, California—would result in several publications. The book quoted here details the ease with which the journey west could be made via the recently completed railroad system. Nordhoff even included the number of days required to visit various places and the current prices for planning your travel budget.

Nordhoff estimated that a first-class five-week tour would take thirty-three days round trip from Chicago and cost about $500. This included the extra fees to change your greenbacks into gold, the only currency used in California. Of course, Yosemite was a "must see" on any traveler's list, and Nordhoff advised an extra week there since the outer rim "can be done by ladies now without discomfort." Once in San Francisco (the only western terminal of the new transcontinental railroads), one could branch out by boat, horseback, stage or private coach to visit the rest of the state. To get clear down to remote Los Angeles, it was best to take a steamer for $18 each way.

Nordhoff was much taken with the potential of the San Bernardino Valley:

> *The valley has not only abundance of running water, constant the year round, but a large number of spouting artesian wells have been bored... You enter the valley after which San Bernardino is named, which, with the adjoining foothills, contains a great tract of first-class farming and orchard land...The old Mission of San Bernardino* [about a mile from Redlands' Asistencia on Barton Road], *now a shapeless ruin, lies high up among the foot-hills.*

By the time frozen easterners finished reading Nordhoff's account of cheap land, miraculous year-round growing conditions and the easy access to this paradise, it is no wonder that they came in droves.

Edith Parker Hinkley, in her book of Redlands history titled *On the Banks of the Zanja*, told how George Beattie came here in 1874. His mother read Nordhoff's book and promptly abandoned Oberlin, Ohio, with her fifteen-year-old son and eighty-one-year-old mother in tow. They bought a small cabin on the corner of Pioneer and Church Streets. The cabin and its twenty acres of land included five shares of South Fork water for a total cost of $476. Astonished friends and family in Ohio grimly predicted that the trip would kill George's grandmother, but she was a living testament to Nordhoff's words and found eight years of health, pleasure and residence in California.

George Beattie was to become the town of Lugonia's first teacher and went on to become a professor and dean at the University of the Philippines. In his later years, he and his wife, Helen, returned to research and write the definitive *History of the San Bernardino Valley.*

The Beatties were part of a wave of settlers with names familiar to Redlanders. Israel Beal and his family moved in down the street. The Reeves family came in 1876, and in 1877, George Cook, E.G. Judson and Frank E. Brown began their historic association with the area.

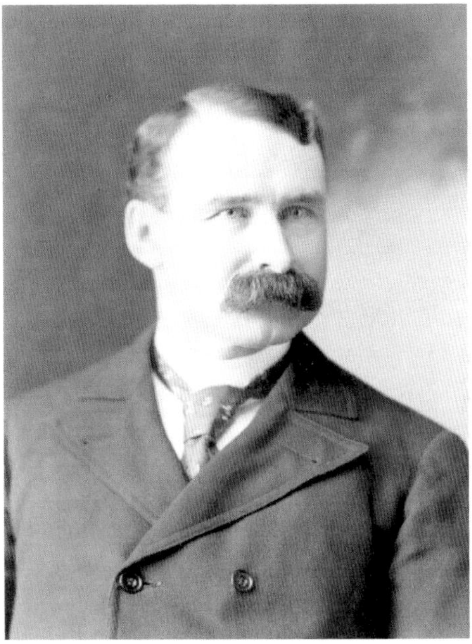

George Beattie was the first teacher at the first Lugonia School. He helped found Pomona College and had a successful career in higher education in the Philippines. In retirement, Beattie and his wife, Helen Pruitt Beattie, researched and wrote *The Heritage of the San Bernardino Valley*, the foundation for all other histories of the area.

The 1870s also saw the rise to eminence of the Crafton Retreat, one of the first health resorts in Southern California. The Myron Crafts family had settled at the upper end of the valley in the 1860s in an area originally known as Eastberne. The Crafts ranch, called Altoona, was located alongside the Zanja at the corner of what is now Colton and Crafton Avenues. It was the sole settlement there for many years, an oasis of green in a sea of brown hills. The tourists who enjoyed the hospitality of Crafton Retreat also saw the possibilities for development in the surrounding area. Soon the Crafts were joined by the Paines, the Caves, the Carpenters, the Willises and Dr. William Craig.

Other areas of Southern California recalled their origins as inspired by Charles Nordhoff. Nordhoff was greatly taken with an area inland from Ventura and Santa Barbara. The town located in this picturesque mountain bowl was named Nordhoff by the proprietors of its first hotel because they had come to California as a result of his book. During World War I, anti-German sentiment was so high that the town was renamed Ojai.

In addition to writing travel books, Nordhoff was a successful journalist and editor of the *New York Herald*. Nordhoff's fortunes increased to the point that he decided to take his own advice. In 1890, Nordhoff persuaded his son, Walter, to drop his own journalism career and leave behind the glitter of his posts in London and Berlin. Charles Nordhoff had purchased fifty thousand acres of land in Baja California two years previously, and he wanted Walter to help him develop a working ranch.

By this circuitous route, Redlands would become "home" to Walter Nordhoff and his succeeding generations.

The City Was Born Below Prospect Park

When Frank E. Brown met Edward G. Judson in 1877, Redlands was thought to be undevelopable. The view from the hills was spectacular, but the only available water was from the Santa Ana River and the Mill Creek Zanja, which flowed through the valley below. It was obvious to all that water would not run uphill.

In the late 1870s and 1880s, winter-weary easterners were being lured to California in droves by legitimate developers and hucksters alike. Brown was a Yale-educated engineer, and Judson was a New York stockbroker. They had the dream and the vision to create a town. They acquired financial backing from Louis Jacobs, a private banker from San Bernardino, and they also did their homework.

Brown and Judson hid their survey equipment in the bottom of a wagon, drove up the long slope we know as Cajon Street and sighted to the point where the Santa Ana River leaves the mountains. From the base of Prospect

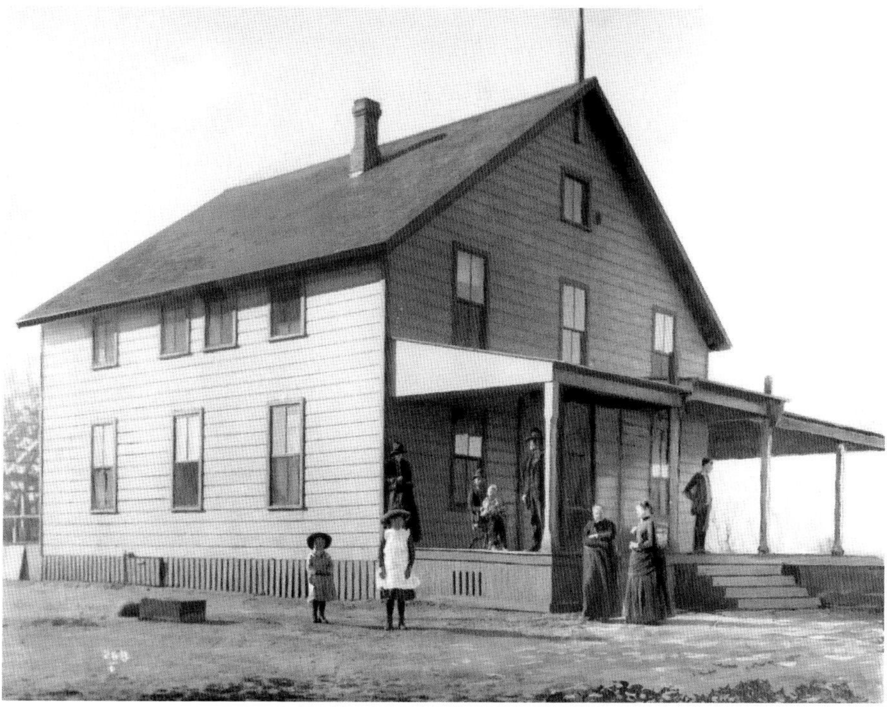

Prospect House was built on a knoll southwest of the corner of Cajon Street and Highland Avenue. Part hotel and part boardinghouse, it was run by Dr. Ellen B. Seymour, a cousin of Frank Brown. For three years, until the completion of the dam project, water had to be hauled in barrels from the Zanja.

Park, approximately the corner of Highland and Cajon, the river was higher. It was obvious to them that water would run quite nicely downhill, and thus Redlands was conceived.

The headquarters for the Redlands Colony was set up in a converted barn above their survey site. The only buildings south of Lugonia were a few squatters' cabins, and there was a need for a place to put up workmen and prospective buyers. In spite of primitive conditions, Judson and Brown's enthusiasm for the project was infectious. Prospect House, as it became known, was often crowded, literally, to the rafters.

Brown's cousin, Dr. Ellen Seymour, became the proprietor of Prospect House. She also tended one and all as Redlands' only physician from 1881 to 1887. It took a while to get the water across the valley, and for three years, all the water for Prospect House had to be hauled in barrels from the Zanja below. The lots began to sell, and Frank Brown began to worry that his fifty shares of South Fork water from the river would not be enough.

Brown and his friend Hiram Barton made their way into the mountains to look at an area known as Bear Valley. Edith Parker Hinckley quoted Brown: "When we first reached the narrow granite gap, at the outlet of the valley, I saw what I had dreamed of for several years, a place specially designed by Providence for a Dam to hold back the winter floods for summer use."

This original Big Bear Dam was built entirely with private funds. Frank Brown made the two-day trip into the mountains time after time to show the site to potential investors. The Bear Valley Land and Water Company was formed in 1883, and the dam was built between June and December 1884. It was a single-arch masonry dam. The curve faced upstream, which directed the pressure to the sides, where the dam ties into the granite edges of the valley. The difficult building process overcame spring floods and the trials of freighting materials and equipment over the desert and mountain ranges. The dam was finished on Frank Brown's twenty-eighth birthday. A higher, multiple-arch dam was completed, slightly downstream, in 1912, but the original structure still stands firm underwater, supporting the roadway that crosses the dam.

Redlands acreage began to sell like hotcakes. Two early visitors were Philadelphia leather tycoon Thomas Y. England and his son, Will. In 1887, the England family became permanent residents of Redlands. They, along with Thomas's wife, E. Clarissa Combs England, joined other early millionaires, who helped establish a tradition of unselfish giving to their new hometown.

England purchased the sixty acres above Highland Avenue that became known as Prospect Park. Unlike the Smiley brothers in Cañon Crest Park, he never built a home there. It is said that Mrs. England thought that the hill

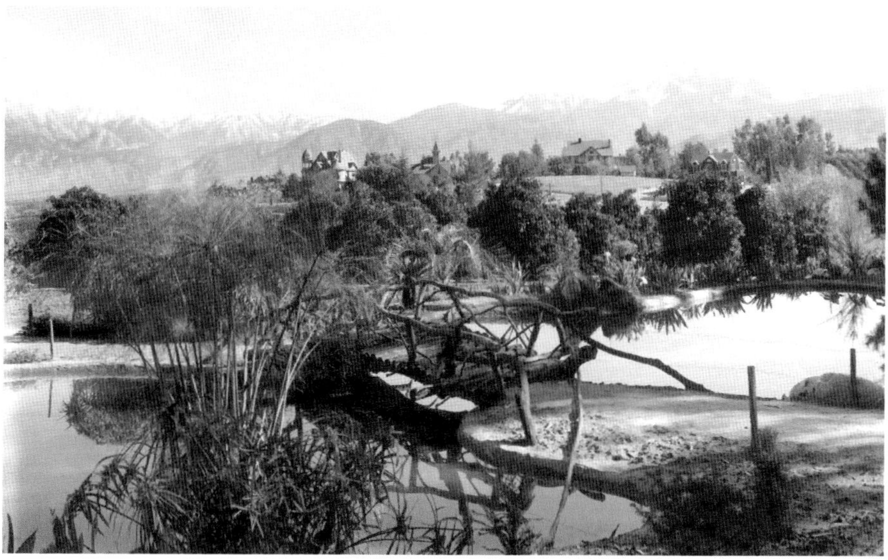

From this now-removed water feature in Prospect Park, you can look across to the next ridge to early homes on Summit Avenue.

up to the park was too steep for the horses and was not interested in living there. The *Daily Facts* reported in 1897 that "Mr. England…has a tasty and commodious residence on Palm Avenue."

The England family followed the lead of the Smiley brothers and transformed their hill, albeit more gradually. During the heyday of the Redlands' tourist era, Prospect Park was an important stop for Tallyho and surrey passengers.

Prospect Park was smaller but similar to Cañon Crest Park. A large pond was created at the high point of the property. Stocked with goldfish, it had a quaint bridge over it. The roadways were sculpted and terraced with stone walls crowned by a profusion of rose bushes. Many rare plants were brought in to provide additional color and interest.

Frank Brown hoped to deliver water from Redlands to develop towns in Moreno Valley. A pipeline brought water through the San Timoteo Canyon hills in 1891. However, the plentiful rainfall that had blessed the years since Big Bear Dam was completed turned dry. The year 1899 had the least measurable rain since records had been kept, and Brown's business failed. The Bear Valley Land and Water Company was forced to reorganize and went into the hands of a receiver. In 1909, the Bear Valley Mutual Water Company emerged from the mess, but Frank Brown was blamed for the catastrophe. It was a sad end for someone so instrumental in developing the town.

Part II
Oranges Fed the Early Years

In 1900, the largest industry in Redlands involved the production of navel oranges. In the short fifty years since the introduction of the navel, the cycles of weather had not produced a recorded freeze, and Redlanders still believed that they were below the frost belt. The city directory extolled: "The temperature in summer rarely exceeds 100 degrees and the lowest point ever reached was 24 degrees, but even then, no harm was done to the fruit."

Early settlers to Southern California had grown the fruits familiar to them as easterners. Apricots, peaches, pears, walnuts, figs, olives, prunes and grapes were planted, harvested and dried for shipment. Fruit drying became a seasonal industry employing many people. Citrus fruits were exotic and scarce until the 1890s, when the first orange trees matured enough to produce a viable crop.

The navel orange introduced in the 1850s by the Van Leuven family thrived in the clay soil of the southern hills, and an industry was born, albeit slowly. By 1897, 400,000 orange trees had been planted, compared with 92,000 grapevines, 34,000 apricot trees, 30,000 peach trees and 18,000 olive trees. Oranges were the lords of the valley. The orange groves provided jobs for pickers, packers and shippers.

The *Citrograph* reported in January 1900: "Conductor Bert Osbun, of the Redlands and San Bernardino motor railway, was at Redlands Junction on Friday of last week when the big Southern Pacific orange train went by. There were fifty-nine cars, drawn by three locomotives, and carrying over

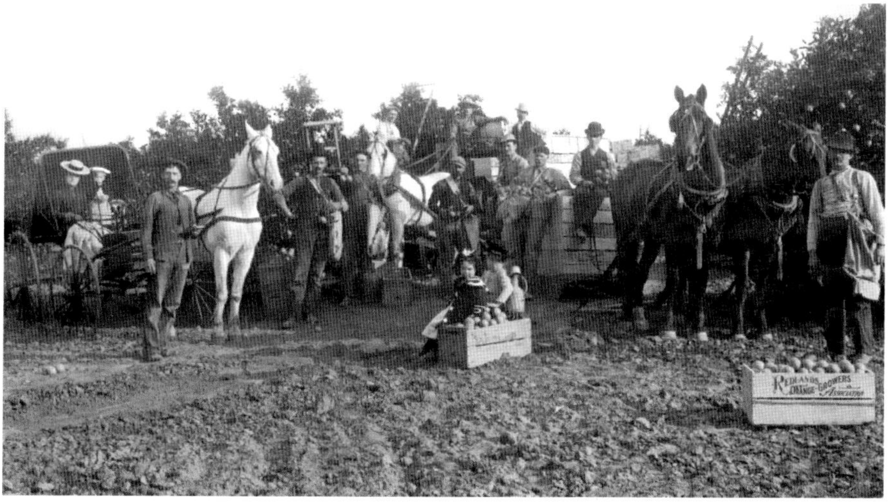

Growing oranges in the early 1900s was a family affair.

22,000 boxes of oranges. This is probably the largest orange train that has ever left California."

The growing local economy provided goods and services of all types. In the January 20, 1900 issue of the *Citrograph*, publisher and Redlands cheerleader Scipio Craig reported that more than $1 million had been spent on dwellings, places of business, school upgrades and churches in the previous year: "This is no stretch of the imagination, and no effort of a boom-inspired writer. Redlands has no boom; Redlands wants no boom; Redlands needs no boom. With the expenditure of a cool million of dollars for materials and labor for absolutely permanent improvements in a single year we are well content with the past and look hopefully forward to the future. Our prosperity is well assured."

Many home sites came with five acres for planting oranges. Five acres of oranges was a generous supplement to a person's income. Ten acres had the promise of sustaining a family and sending the kids to college. If you drive south on Center or San Mateo Streets, you will notice the occasional grove cottage hemmed in by newer houses where the groves once were. The cross streets—Palm, Cypress and Fern—each still have some groves that show what it was like one hundred years ago. Olive Avenue, by contrast, is populated with turn-of-the-century homes elbow to elbow, having been designated residential from the beginning.

The realities of weather and the allure of dollars offered by land developers eventually led to the demise of the family grove. In 1913, the year of the

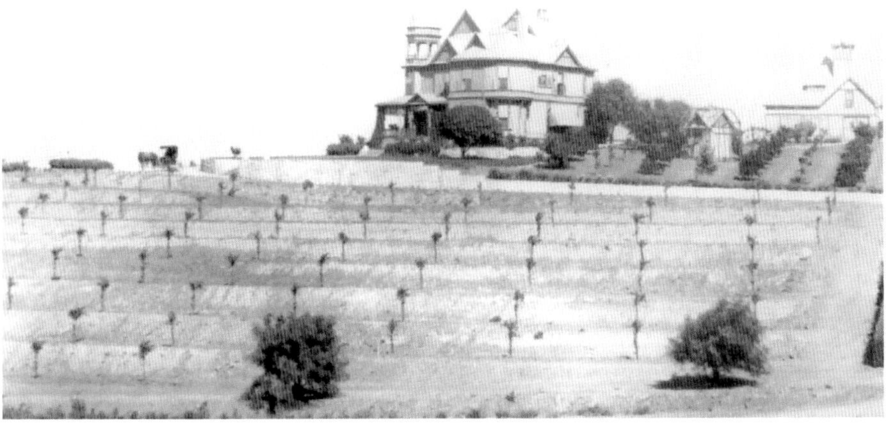

The Eldrige M. Lyon House in 1889 shows the beginnings of a Victorian home in the groves.

Big Freeze, the temperature dropped to eighteen degrees. Not only was the orange crop ruined, many trees were split as well. Electricity fizzled because the water froze on its way to the generating plant. The orange industry was sharply curtailed, and Redlands' economy was affected for a decade.

A similar freeze fifty years later, in 1963, had a less devastating affect on local employment and the economy, but within a month after the latter freeze, building permits totaled more than $2 million, and housing projects expanded, filling in the spaces formerly held by orange trees.

Lord Orange's days were numbered—one packinghouse remains where there were once more than ninety. In recent years, a bond measure has given the city of Redlands the ability to purchase orange groves. These groves provide a link to the past and a green belt to soften development. In addition, civic groups have joined to plant new groves to beautify the entrances to the city.

The economy may have diversified—Redlands' largest employers are now healthcare providers, education and software developers—but the orange remains foremost in our hearts. Though we now know it can be frosty, we are still proud to be part of the "citrus belt."

Rail System Was Important Factor in Early City Growth

The 1880s produced a boom decade for Southern California. For one three-month period in 1887, agents for the railroads, along with professional promoters, fueled a real estate orgy that resulted in the laying out of thirteen new town sites between Los Angeles and San Bernardino.

E.G. Judson and Frank Brown bought the first 320 acres of what would become the new town of Redlands from the Southern Pacific Railroad in 1881. Once Judson and Brown had solved the water supply problem with the development of a reservoir in Bear Valley (now known as Big Bear Lake), they could turn their attention to the difficulties of transportation. A stagecoach line connected Redlands to a Southern Pacific siding in San Timoteo Canyon, but our founders understood that growth would be limited until there was a railway to get people and goods in and out of the town center.

Like so many other public works of the day, the railroad was brought to Redlands by private sponsorship instead of government funding. William G. Moore, in *Redlands Yesterdays*, wrote:

> *Redlands' development program called for railroads, main lines preferably, as many as possible, as quickly as possible. A Santa Fe branch, the California Southern, would arrive if Redlands would present it with a paid-for right-of-way from San Bernardino. Under aggressive canvassing by R.J. Waters and E.G. Judson, Redlands (with fewer than a thousand residents) raised $42,750, probably the largest per capita bonus ever given any railroad. By February 1888, the Santa Fe was serving Redlands.*

The year 1888 also saw the beginning of streetcar service in Redlands. The Redlands Street Railway's mule-drawn cars lasted until 1898. This first streetcar service extended from State and Orange Streets, up Cajon and west on Highland Avenue to Center Street.

The two mules had to be replaced every two trips. Sometimes the mules had difficulty with the grade, and passengers had to get out and push. The cars were open on the sides and featured storm curtains for protection against the weather and the all-pervasive dust kicked up from the unpaved streets. Motorman Phil Dreiser was the mule driver for ten years. He cheerfully ran errands for housewives along the route and transported hundreds of patrons for a fare of five cents.

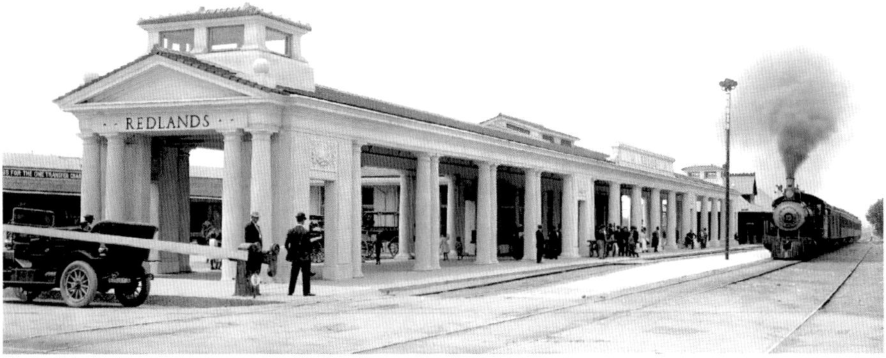

The Santa Fe Depot in downtown Redlands opened the city to the world. Several trains a day transported residents to Los Angeles, brought winter residents and saw thousands of tourists arrive to take the tour of Cañon Crest Park.

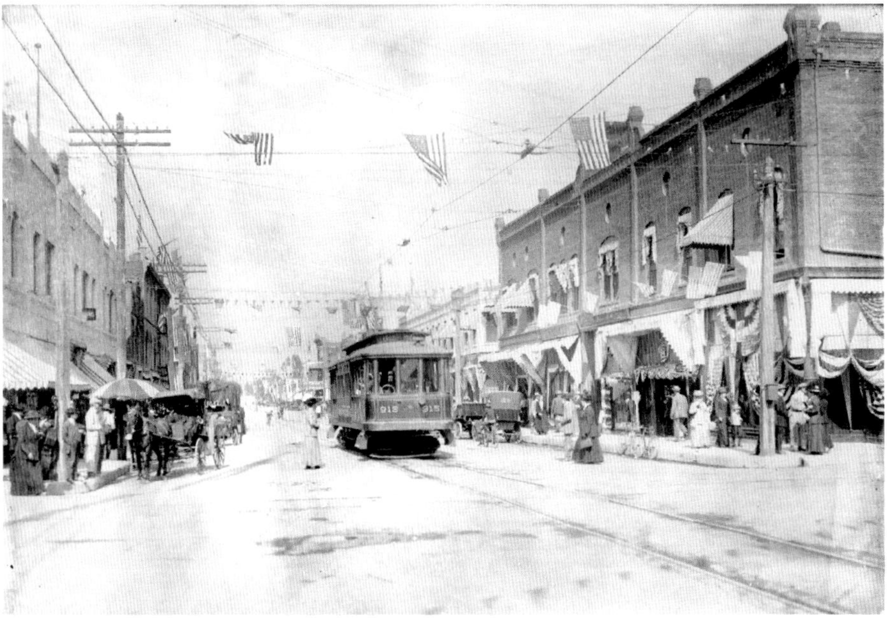

A network of electric streetcars replaced the mule-drawn ones after electricity became available in the late 1890s.

The upgrade to electricity was delayed by the depression of the mid-1890s, to the point that Scipio Craig, the colorful editor of the *Citrograph*, began calling the service "Redlands Snailways…the antiquated shell that has been dragged over that line by fourteen generations of mules and mulettes since the town's start…running on the same uneven track, the same elliptical wheels, and driven by the same gentleman."

Modernization finally came, and at its height, the streetcar system was quite extensive. Lines ran from Lugonia Avenue along Orange, up Cajon to the Country Club, and even had a special double track in front of the Wyatt Opera House at Orange and Colton, so that cars queued up to take theatergoers home would not interrupt regular service.

Additional lines ran along Cypress to Center, up Center to Cedar and over to Serpentine, through the orchards below Smiley Heights to Terracina and back Olive to Cajon. You could also ride from Brookside and San Mateo to Citrus and then east to Wabash. Edith Parker Hinckley told a story of the streetcar drivers and their influence over the citizens of the day: "The motormen rather lorded it over the preachers, for if the churches were not out by twelve o'clock Sunday noon the bells would clang and people would get up and go out. This encouraged the ministers of Redlands to give short sermons!"

Sadly for us, the last streetcar run was in 1936. The automobile was king. I wonder what it will take to get the rails back. Perhaps if we all get out and push?

In Sickness and Health: How Invalids Influenced Redlands

J.S. Edwards was sent to Southern California in 1881 to die. He reported in 1929 that he "still expected to die if his life was spared."

–*Edith Parker Hinckley,* On the Banks of the Zanja

For the first time in history a frontier was settled by invalids.

–*L.E. Nelson,* Only One Redlands

In the years of early Redlands, tuberculosis (or consumption, as it was commonly known) was a serious threat to the health of the entire country. A report from the local board of health covering the year ending June 1, 1895, showed that thirty-six of the seventy-two deaths in Redlands were due to consumption. Of those deaths, all but three were invalids hoping to prolong their lives by coming to Redlands to live. Two of the other three were nurses infected by their charges. A full 25 percent of the population died from tuberculosis. There was no known cure, and people were just beginning to understand the way it spread.

As I have read through the different accounts of Redlands' development, I have been struck by how many of our founding fathers (and mothers) came here for health reasons. Most of these soon-to-be-well-known invalids came with enough wealth to buy land and undertake new enterprises as their health improved. Many were quite young, their education interrupted or unused, as their parents sent them to the Southwest in the hopes that the dry climate would provide a cure.

Fortunately, many survived the disease. We know today that rest and healthy diet prolonged and sometimes cured a patient of tuberculosis. Long before the days of antibiotics, doctors could diagnose the disease, but they were unable to predict the cure. Stories of the day are a mixture of sensible prevention and quackery.

Nelson, in his book, *Only One Redlands*, devoted a chapter to "In Hope of Health":

> *Slowly the world, including Redlands, became aware of the tuberculosis bacillus and the dangers of its spread through sputum.*
>
> *Redlands became very health conscious. The city ordered rotting weeds cleaned from reservoirs every three months, urged boiling of drinking water, tried to keep sheep, both alive and dead, out of the Santa Ana and the Zanja. It became finicky about fertilizer draining from groves into drinking water. It planted corn in the sewer farm on Texas Street.*

Evidently, corn reduced the odors from the sewage. Sunflowers were thought to be even better and were planned for the next season. City gutters were an unrecognized problem for several years. Flies were not mentioned, and people took a chance drinking unpasteurized milk, even though it was a known carrier of the tuberculosis bacillus.

Fumigation procedures were put into place. An anti-spitting ordinance was passed, and the ladies of the Contemporary Club took the opportunity to join the national society for the abolition of the chewing gum habit.

More from Nelson:

> [T]*he state made vaccination compulsory for school children, who were warned against shared use of pens and pencils.*
>
> *Redlands Methodists and Congregationalists incurred the wrath of many of their co-religionists elsewhere by their…innovation, individual communion cups. Not until 1910, however, were public school drinking*

cups cast out, drinking fountains installed, and individual towels and soap planned for the pupils.

The new town was faced with a real dilemma: encourage the growth and development that was bringing fame and wealth to the area or pull in its horns and hide from disease. Even the acquisition of new city parks became debatable because people feared that consumptives would sit in them and cough.

The topic was talked about in whispers until one memorable city council meeting. A minister member, a known prohibitionist, declared openly that he would rather see three new saloons open than an increase in the number of consumptives coming to town. This caused quite a panic in the meeting, as other members were afraid that the press would pick up on his comments. "Better not discuss consumption for publication," it was said.

Medicine shows, miracle cures and gadgets were advertised liberally in the newspapers. Some of my favorites: the California Positive and Negative Electric Cough and Consumption Cure; William Radam's Microbe Killer (99.381 percent water plus hydrochloric and sulfuric acids, colored with red wine); and Dr. A.J. Shores' Grand Free Medicine Show ("If you can't laugh don't come").

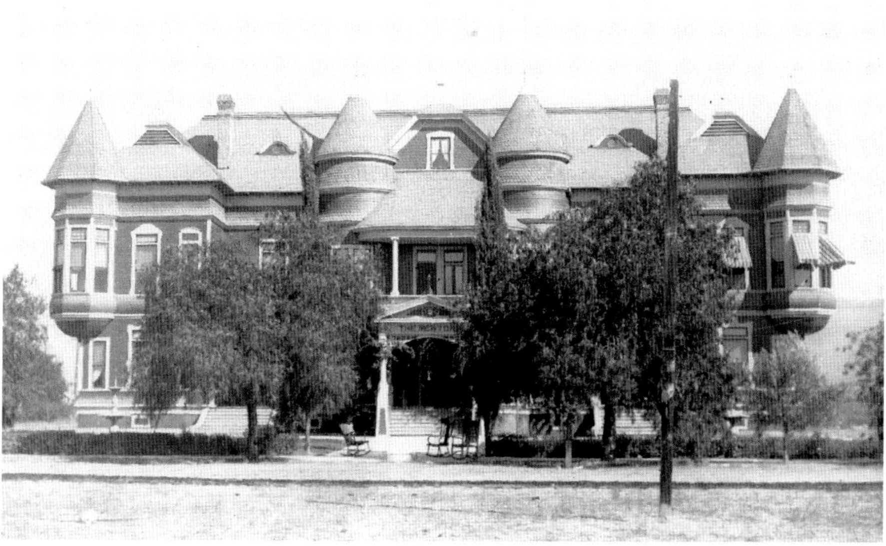

At one time, eight trains a day brought tourists and resortgoers to the Mentone Sanatorium at the farthest stop of the Santa Fe Railroad's kite-shaped track.

The controversial draw of a sanitarium divided the town. Eventually, one was opened in Mentone and another, Trinity Settlement, in San Timoteo Canyon. The latter was supported by Trinity Episcopal Church and was the first of its kind in Southern California.

The search for health created architectural side benefits. Our turn-of-the-century homes owe their large windows, sleeping porches and airy parlors to the quest for clean air.

I wonder if the anti-spitting ordinance is still on the books.

Calling the Doctor in Early Redlands, Often Via Heliograph

Into his mind came the memory of something he had read of the heliograph, and of methods of signaling with mirrors.

–*Harold Bell Wright,* The Eyes of the World

The heliograph, hmm? In *The Smileys*, by Larry E. Burgess, there is a reference to signaling with mirrors as a means to communicate between the Smiley homes in Redlands and their mountain resort, Fredalba, near the top of what is now Highway 330.

Research tells me that several armies employed heliographs, using mirrors to signal Morse code, during the late 1800s. Wright's reference to the heliograph describes the novel's protagonist employing mirrors to request the delivery of supplies for his high-altitude camp. He signals from his mountain perch and is answered from the orange groves of Fairlands (based on Redlands).

The heliograph actually played a part in the delivery of medical care to the mountain communities surrounding Redlands before the advent of rural telephones. In these days of antibiotics, it is easy to forget the daily impact that illness had on the lives of those living before penicillin. Diaries written in the late 1800s and early 1900s are filled with worried entries regarding the health of loved ones. The Nordhoff diaries found in the Heritage Room of the A.K. Smiley Library are no exception.

Walter Nordhoff, one of the wealthy residents who built lavish homes in turn-of-the-century Redlands, chronicled a privileged lifestyle tinged with constant concern. Though his references to the frequent small illnesses befalling his family members might seem like hypochondriacal melodrama today, they were expressions of real fear. Influenza often lead to pneumonia and death; a small cut or broken bone that became infected was curable only by time and the grace of God. Injury and illness had no more respect for the wealthy than they did for the poor.

Many families, rich and poor, came to Southern California because of tuberculosis. The mostly healthy Nordhoffs were an exception. Among the invalids were names familiar to those interested in the history of our town: Edwards, Fisk, Ford, Kingsbury, Sinclair and Fisher are but a few.

L.E. Nelson, in *Only One Redlands*, wrote: "In 1892 a physician reported that at least eight out of ten of Southern California's clergy, dentists, doctors and lawyers originally came for their health. By 1900 California led the country in doctors per capita, leading a wag to wonder whether the large number of doctors in California was due to the great number of invalids or vice versa."

One such doctor was Walter Bonhomie Power. Dr. Power arrived in Redlands in 1902. Only twenty-seven years old, Dr. Power had already made a name for himself in New York. He was an instructor of anatomy at Columbia, as well as house surgeon at Bellevue Hospital. Unfortunately, Power had shared a house with some friends, and their tuberculosis-infected butler had in turn infected all of them.

Power decided to "take the cure" in Redlands and was one of the lucky ones who recovered. He established a medical practice and became friends with the Nordhoff family, especially Charlie, who was about five years younger than Power. (This is the Charles Nordhoff who later paired with James Norman Hall to write several novels, including *Mutiny on the Bounty*.) Power would often accompany Charlie or his younger brother, Franklin, on local hunting and fishing trips.

In addition to his Redlands medical practice, Power kept a practice in Big Bear. Making house calls in Big Bear from Redlands would be a challenge today. Power's story is the stuff of legends.

Before 1915 or so, the shortest route to Big Bear Lake from Redlands could be accomplished on horseback in about five or six hours. The lowest part traversed the Southern California Power Company's road up lower Santa Ana Canyon. From there, it zigzagged steeply up the divide between the Santa Ana River and Bear Valley and down to the lake. It was a sort of as-the-crow-flies route that required four changes of horses along the way.

Power's son, Stuart, told me of the time his dad got an early morning call to deliver a baby in Big Bear. He headed up the mountain at 6:00 a.m. and arrived about 11:00 a.m. He checked on the expectant Mom and found

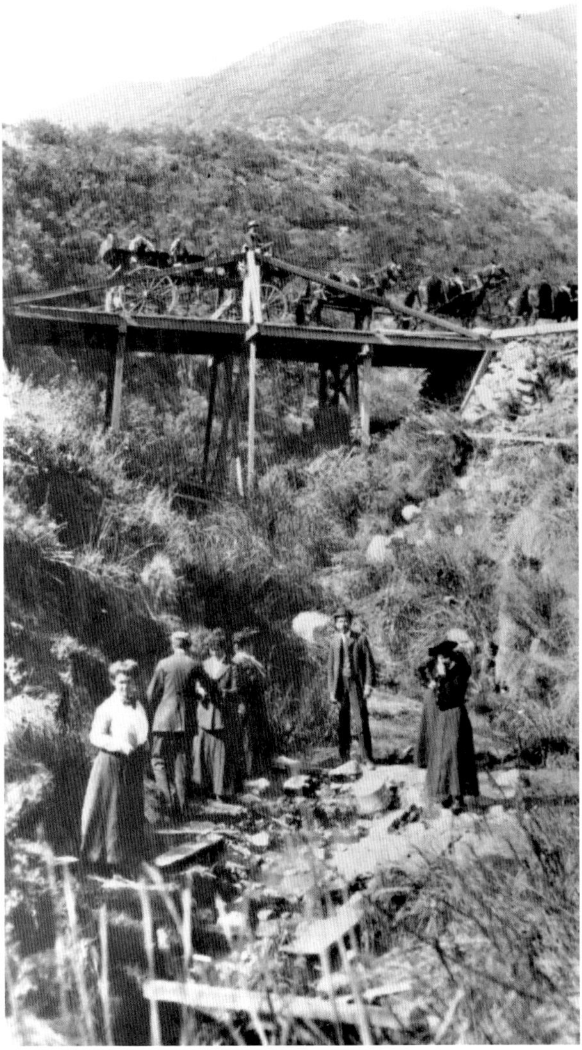

A trip up the mountains through the Santa Ana Canyon was arduous and involved several changes of horses.

her not ready to birth, so he went fishing for a few hours, delivered the baby at about five o'clock that evening and was just settling down to stay overnight when word came that he was needed in Redlands. Back on horseback at 6:00 p.m., he returned down the mountain, saw his patient at the Nordina Street Hospital about midnight and performed surgery the next morning.

From our vantage point today, it sounds quite normal to say, "The doctor got a call." In fact, Redlands has had telephone service since the 1890s, but service to Big Bear was another matter. The area we now know as Big Bear City was called Pine Knot in those days. Somewhere above Pine Knot was a place on the ridge that had a clear view of the valley floor. Dr. Power's calls came in the form of a heliograph.

I wonder what one of today's health insurers would do with a claim that involved horseback and heliograph?

Building a High School Was Never Easy

In 1891, the *Ontario Record* printed a scathing comment directed at Redlands: "The only union high school organized in this county is that…of the districts of Redlands, Lugonia, and Crafton. The…tax for high school purposes… will be thirty-two cents on the hundred dollars. That makes a high school a pretty expensive luxury."

Citrograph editor Scipio Craig responded on October 3, 1891: "When it comes to the question of educating our children at home or sending them abroad the former 'goes' every time, no matter what has become synonymous with intelligence, education, culture and refinement, and the synonymousness will be kept up, for our people are proud of their reputation."

By 1891, the area had three school districts: Lugonia, Crafton and Redlands. The combined school population had swelled to five hundred pupils. High school students had to attend one of the few private schools in the area or go off to boarding school. A new state law allowed districts to consolidate for their high school needs, and Redlands was the first community in the state to do so. In 1891, the three districts formed the Redlands Union High School District and began to look for a site.

The September 19, 1891 *Citrograph* reported that the board of trustees wasted no time in making the decision to open a temporary high school in a building on the Terrace on October 1: "The hall will be divided into two rooms and fitted up in handsome shape. The expense of operating the school this present year is estimated at $6,000."

It was voted to extend the principal's contract to Professor H.F. Wegener, a graduate of Chicago Medical College. He was described as forty-six years old, with a wife and three children, "a man of commanding presence." He had taught for twenty-four years and was "most qualified" in science, English, mathematics, civil government and German. The board approved a salary of $1,700 per year.

The trustees reviewed ten possible building sites for the high school's permanent location. They decided on a four-and-a-half-acre lot at Church and High Streets (directly under the current roadbed of the I-10). The controversy over the selection of the site presaged the objections raised over the location of Redlands' second high school, Redlands East Valley, with one main difference. In 1891, Redlands voters rejected the bond issue for a high school because they feared that the neighborhood noise would be too great for the students. The site was located next to the railroad tracks. Late twentieth-century complaints about Redlands East

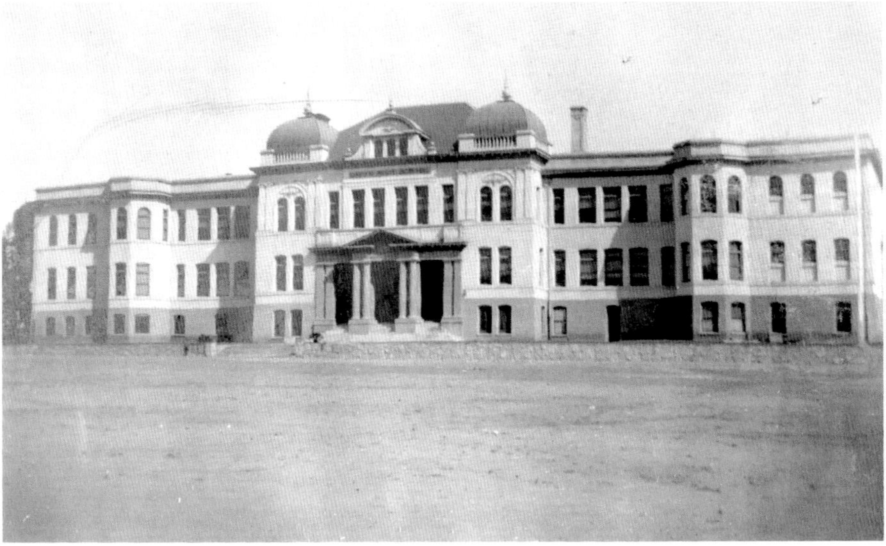

Redlands Union High School, built in 1892, was designed by T.R. Griffith, the architect of the A.K. Smiley Public Library.

Valley swirled around fears that the students would be too noisy for the neighborhood.

Redlands voters' pride in their community was evident six weeks later as they approved a new bond issue for $17,000 ($5,000 higher than the rejected one). The difference was a quieter location in the bog of a former brickyard at Citrus and Church. In September 1892, the board of trustees requested bids for the new building. The architect for the Redlands Post Office, T.R. Griffith, designed an imposing two-story brick building with four rooms and a basement, to be built on the corner of Reservoir Road (now Roosevelt Road) and Fern Avenue.

The bid was awarded to contractor F.E. Lynn, who broke ground one month later. I guess the plans didn't have to be approved by Sacramento.

To quote L.E. Nelson:

> *Ironically, the selected site proved…the noisiest one in all Redlands. First it was the back-firing from loaded trucks descending Citrus from Oak Glen. Then on the opposite side, Roosevelt Road and Highway 99, with campus crashing of runaway trucks unable to make the sharp turn. In 1962, the noise diminished slightly, the new freeway being a block away.*

Cheers now to Redlands High School, Redlands East Valley High School and Citrus Valley High School. May you live long and prosper quietly, the town enhanced by your presence and not diminished, producing new generations of citizens proud of their reputation.

Family Service Helps Redlanders Help Themselves

It is nice to be reminded that one of Redlands' oldest institutions is one whose purpose has always been "to alleviate poverty and encourage self-sufficiency." Some might say it got off to a rocky start.

The financial panic of 1893 and its ensuing depression sent droves of unemployed workers west to seek their fortunes. For those who hopped the Southern Pacific Railroad through San Gorgonio Pass, the first stop past the desert and mountains was at the mouth of San Timoteo Canyon; the closest town was Redlands.

City services were stretched to the max trying to keep pace with the fast-developing town. The appearance of beggars on the street and homeless on park benches was a problem that the local police was not equipped to handle. In early 1895, Albert Smiley, led by his belief that a person should earn his way in the world and not be given a handout, proposed an opportunity for unemployed drifters. They could exchange three hours' labor for a meal ticket from a local restaurant. The catch? The three hours must be spent pounding large rocks into usable pieces.

On November 23, 1895, the *Citrograph* reported that "the county supervisors have ordered the sheriff to give tramps a clearance card on their discharge from the county rock pile. The card shall secure immunity from arrest for four days to allow them to get out of the county. The rock pile will prevent their ever coming back of their own free will."

The rock pile was meant to apply to transients, not the resident poor of the city. Thank goodness that Albert's twin brother, Alfred, had a separate vision for them. The Smiley brothers came to Redlands in their retirement years, but they were never retired. They worked ceaselessly for the improvement and promotion of their adopted town. Though not as wealthy as many of their Redlands contemporaries, the twins set a philanthropic tone for the rest to follow.

In February 1898, Alfred Smiley persuaded the Minister's Association to call a meeting, which resulted in the formation of the Associated Charities

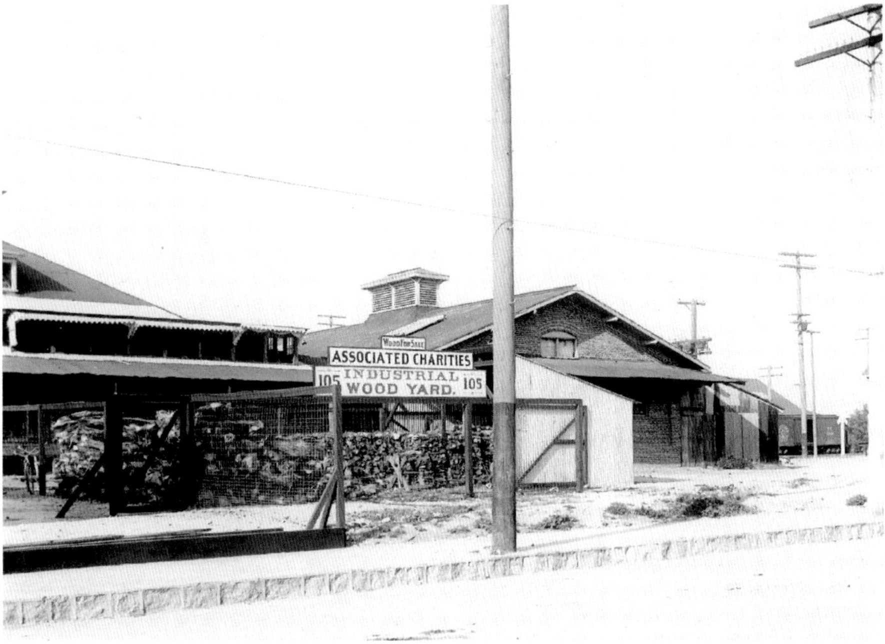

Associated Charities was created by a group of citizens in 1898, with Alfred Smiley as its first president. With a mission to provide temporary assistance, "a hand up, not a handout," this lumberyard provided jobs to out-of-work local citizens. Associated Charities became Family Service Association of Redlands in celebration of its fiftieth anniversary in 1948. For more than one hundred years, Family Service has continued to serve those in need in the community.

(known as Family Service Association of Redlands since 1948). It was founded on the same "no handouts" principle as Albert Smiley's rock pile, but there the resemblance ended. Interested donors were asked to meet minimum dues of $0.25 per month, which entitled them to be called subscribers. The first month brought in $102.00, of which $70.83 was authorized to be spent.

Until 1904, volunteers ran the organization. Subscribers would divide up the caseload and offer whatever assistance they could. As the load grew, an executive secretary was hired. Half of her job was to collect from procrastinating subscribers, and half was to act as visiting missionary.

Eldridge Lyon (who gave the Lyon Wing of the Smiley Library) purchased and donated the building at 114 West Vine Street to Family Service in 1932. The organization operated from there until 1987, when it moved to West Colton Avenue.

In the early years, aid was dispensed on a first come/first serve basis. Limited resources and the location in downtown Redlands produced a modest caseload.

In addition to food, clothing and financial assistance, a visiting nurse made her rounds on a regular and "as-needed" basis. In 1962, 402 families were served by the nurse, grocery orders (available once a month), Christmas Shop, Thanksgiving and Christmas baskets and Clothing Room. The budget was about $15,000. By 1972, the visiting nurse was gone. She was replaced by five social workers who provided an evening counseling program. The budget had doubled to $30,000, and 752 families were served.

In 1920, the Presbyterian church organized the House of Neighborly Services. In 1994, the Redlands House of Neighborly Services, and its Home Again Project, merged with the Family Service Association of Redlands. Located at 612 Lawton Street, housing programs from Home Again are funded by grants and donations. In 2004, the Lawton Street location was enlarged, and the operations of Family Service and Home Again were combined on the property.

Current Family Service staff and volunteers are understandably proud of the accomplishments of their organization. The Home Again Project is the only program in the area that aims to actually solve the problems of the homeless. It is not a giveaway program but rather a comprehensive approach that helps families get back on their feet and into permanent housing and helps them keep that housing.

Family Service's other projects are equally successful. The Christmas Shop provides food baskets and gifts for families every year. The Good Samaritan Fund provides interest-free loans for education, emergency mortgage payments and a variety of other needs. Its success is evident in the fact that almost every dollar loaned out has been paid back in full. Parenting and life skills classes are offered.

Family Service's individualized approach continues to attract dedicated volunteers from the community, including many former beneficiaries of its services. Its many community partners continue to help it grow. And they've figured out how to do it without the rock pile.

Unsung Rockwell Eleven Was Really the Best Team in SoCal

A conference championship is an honor sought by every football team as they begin a new season. The fledgling University of Redlands football team won its first Southern California Intercollegiate Athletic Conference Championship in the school year 1918–19 and played one of its strangest games in the process. The tale involves the military, munitions and masks. Armed guards kept the public away from the game, and the opponents arrived two by two, by air. It was an unusual beginning to an unusual season.

The world had been at war since 1914. President Wilson's attempts to keep the United States out of the conflict finally failed, and the country began drafting soldiers to send to France in June 1917. By the fall of 1918, the draft was in full swing, and most of the University of Redlands' remaining male students over the age of seventeen were members of the Student Army Training Corps (SATC).

An insidious virus had hit the trenches in Europe the past summer and was invading the United States. The great influenza pandemic would spread worldwide and ultimately kill between 400,000 and 500,000 people in the United States alone, far more than the 53,000 American lives lost in World War I.

In Redlands, public schools and churches were closed for most of the month of October and into November. Store hours were restricted to daylight, movie and billiard halls were closed and authorities called for a "noiseless Halloween" in order not to disturb the sick. Football schedules announced in September for the Redlands High School and University of Redlands teams were put on indefinite postponement. Even practice was forbidden.

Finally, the University of Redlands proclaimed that the first game of the season would be played on October 26, 1918, against the Rockwell Field Eleven, from San Diego. The *Daily Facts* reported that the "Aviators have a strong team." Six-year Redlands coach Lieutenant Ashel Cunningham bravely responded that the Bulldogs had a large quantity of good material and that he looked forward to the chance to "look 'em over."

The *Facts* noted the obvious: "The fact the University Team has thus far had no practice will work a hardship in the game." The outlook for the Bulldogs was further clouded by the news that they had only a handful of returning players. The Rockwells, however, seemed to be stocked with former all-Americans.

The Rockwell coach, Lieutenant Barett, was a former American League baseball player and former college head football coach. Manager Lieutenant Snyder was a Syracuse University player picked by Yale football coach and father of American football Walter Camp for an all-star team. Lieutenant Carson, the captain, was a Yale all-American, and Lieutenant Fern, the quarterback, was from the University of California. And that is just part of the list.

The October 23, 1918 issue of *The Campus*, the University of Redlands' student newspaper, announced with relief that SATC men would be eligible to play football.

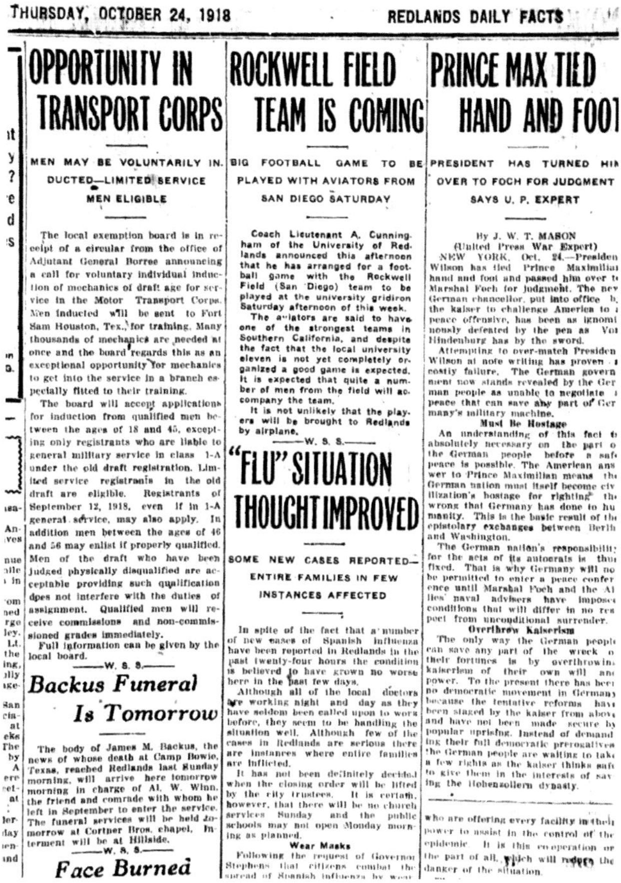

THURSDAY, OCTOBER 24, 1918 REDLANDS DAILY FACTS

OPPORTUNITY IN TRANSPORT CORPS

MEN MAY BE VOLUNTARILY INDUCTED—LIMITED SERVICE MEN ELIGIBLE

The local exemption board is in receipt of a circular from the office of Adjutant General Borree announcing a call for voluntary individual induction of mechanics of draft age for service in the Motor Transport Corps. Men inducted will be sent to Fort Sam Houston, Tex., for training. Many thousands of mechanics are needed at once and the board regards this as an exceptional opportunity for mechanics to get into the service in a branch especially fitted to their training.

The board will accept applications for induction from qualified men between the ages of 18 and 45, excepting only registrants who are liable to general military service in class 1-A under the old draft registration. Limited service registrants in the old draft are eligible. Registrants of September 12, 1918, even if in 1-A general service, may also apply. In addition men between the ages of 46 and 56 may enlist if properly qualified. Men of the draft who have been judged physically disqualified are acceptable providing such qualification does not interfere with the duties of assignment. Qualified men will receive commissions and non-commissioned grades immediately.

Full information can be given by the local board.

—W. S. S.—

Backus Funeral Is Tomorrow

The body of James M. Backus, the news of whose death at Camp Bowie, Texas, reached Redlands last Sunday morning, will arrive here tomorrow morning in charge of Al. W. Winn, the friend and comrade with whom he left in September to enter the service. The funeral services will be held tomorrow at Cortner Bros. chapel. Interment will be at Hillside.

—W. S. S.—

Face Burned

ROCKWELL FIELD TEAM IS COMING

BIG FOOTBALL GAME TO BE PLAYED WITH AVIATORS FROM SAN DIEGO SATURDAY

Coach Lieutenant A. Cunningham of the University of Redlands announced this afternoon that he has arranged for a football game with the Rockwell Field (San Diego) team to be played at the university gridiron Saturday afternoon of this week.

The aviators are said to have one of the strongest teams in Southern California, and despite the fact that the local university eleven is not yet completely organized a good game is expected. It is expected that quite a number of men from the field will accompany the team.

It is not unlikely that the players will be brought to Redlands by airplane.

—W. S. S.—

"FLU" SITUATION THOUGHT IMPROVED

SOME NEW CASES REPORTED—ENTIRE FAMILIES IN FEW INSTANCES AFFECTED

In spite of the fact that a number of new cases of Spanish influenza have been reported in Redlands in the past twenty-four hours the condition is believed to have grown no worse here in the past few days.

Although all of the local doctors are working night and day as they have seldom been called upon to work before, they seem to be handling the situation well. Although few of the cases in Redlands are serious there are instances where entire families are inflicted.

It has not been definitely decided when the closing order will be lifted by the city trustees. It is certain, however, that there will be no church services Sunday and the public schools may not open Monday morning as planned.

Wear Masks

Following the request of Governor Stephens that citizens combat the spread of Spanish influenza by wear-

PRINCE MAX TIED HAND AND FOO

PRESIDENT HAS TURNED HI OVER TO FOCH FOR JUDGMENT SAYS U. P. EXPERT

By J. W. T. MASON
(United Press War Expert)

NEW YORK, Oct. 24.—Presiden Wilson has tied Prince Maximilia hand and foot and passed him over t Marshal Foch for judgment. The ne German chancellor, put into office b the kaiser to challenge America to peace offensive, has been as ignomi niously defeated by the pen as Vo Hindenburg has by the sword.

Attempting to over-match Presiden Wilson at note writing has proven costly failure. The German govern ment now stands revealed by the Ger man people as unable to negotiate peace that can save any part of Ger many's military machine.

Must Be Hostage

An understanding of this fact i absolutely necessary on the part o the German people before a saf peace is possible. The American ans wer to Prince Maximilian means th German nation must itself become civ ilization's hostage for righting th wrong that Germany has done to hu manity. This is the basic result of th epistolary exchanges between Berli and Washington.

The German nation's responsibilit for the acts of its autocrats is thu fixed. That is why Germany will no be permitted to enter a peace confer ence until Marshal Foch and the Al lies' naval advisers have impose conditions that will differ in no res pect from unconditional surrender.

Overthrow Kaiserism

The only way the German peopl can save any part of the wreck o their fortunes is by overthrowin kaiserism of their own will an power. To the present there has bee no democratic movement in German because the tentative reforms hav been staged by the kaiser from abov and have not been made secure b popular uprising. Instead of demand ing their full democratic prerogative the German people are waiting to tak a few rights as the kaiser thinks saf to give them in the interests of sav ing the Hohenzollern dynasty.

who are offering every facility in thei power to assist in the control of th epidemic. It is this co-operation or the part of all, which will reduce th danger of the situation.

The October 26, 1918 *Redlands Daily Facts* announces the University of Redlands v. Rockwell Field football game. The 1919 *La Letra* yearbook summed up the game this way: "Rockwell Field held us down to a goose egg in a football game. No wonder, our fellows could not resist searching for the pigskin in the air; while the aviators were satisfied with being on the sod for a while."

Two days before the big event, Redlands mayor A.E. Brock issued an order that the public would not be allowed to attend the game due to the flu. The game would be played with military guards at the gate.

On Saturday, October 26, the *Daily Facts* headlined: "Football Team to Fly Here for Game This Afternoon." The story continues to describe the excitement of eleven airplanes landing in the vacant field next to the athletic field. The athletic field was located where the Armacost Library and Hunsaker Student Center are now, so the landing would have been on a grassy area to the east now occupied by the Lewis, Appleton and Hedco Halls. Rockwell Field was the birthplace of both U.S. naval and army aviation, and most of the players were cadet aviators. Each plane held two flyers; the rest of the team travelled to Redlands by automobile to round out a group of thirty-four.

The *Daily Facts* reported that

> *the planes arrived one at a time with ten on the ground by 1 o'clock, the eleventh was late in leaving and didn't arrive until late. There were no difficulties with the trip. The aviators followed the coast as far as possible before turning inland.*
>
> *The flight was made in less than two hours and a half, a landing being made in Riverside for gas. New parts were secured for the plane which was injured in landing, enabling it to leave with the main group Sunday morning.*

After landing, the machines were covered with tarps, and members of the SATC were posted as guards. The aviators were taken to the Nichewaug Hotel on Colton Avenue.

The game was played at 3:30 p.m. The Rockwells, dressed out in leather helmets and black sweaters, seemingly none the worse for wear from their flight, scored the first touchdown in less than four minutes. A fumble on the five-yard line in the second quarter spoiled Redlands' best chance to score. The final score was 20–0, and *The Campus* gamely commented that it had been "good practice."

The *Daily Facts* reported that a good crowd turned out to watch both the landing and the Sunday morning takeoff, the highlight of which was the performance of several spectacular aerial stunts by one Lieutenant James Doolittle.

Photos in the 1919 *La Letra* (University of Redlands yearbook) capture the flavor of the events. The two most interesting planes were the one called the *Hun*, decorated with skull and crossbones and a German cross, and the one previously mentioned as "injured" upon landing. The injuries appear to have snapped the plane in half: its tail and wings rest on the ground and its nose waves at an unlikely angle in the air.

The game itself was open only to masked University of Redlands students and faculty, but "no small number of townspeople found positions on the fence and at convenient knot holes."

As for the rest of the season, Redlands defeated Occidental and presumably its other scheduled opponents, Los Angeles Normal College and the Sherman Institute, and took a forfeit from Pomona College (the flu again) to win the Southern California Intercollegiate Athletic Conference. A disappointing loss to the University of Southern California on Christmas Day left the winner of the Southern California championship undecided. I'm guessing the Rockwell Eleven were not considered in the running.

Redlands Produced Race Cars and Oranges

My father-in-law likes to say that the three best things about living in Redlands are January, February and March. It sure beats the frozen memories I have of my childhood in Missouri.

Shortly after writing about the influenza epidemic of 1918, I received a note from Redlands High School's former track and field coach, Bob Scholton. He included a clipping from the *Los Angeles Times*, dated October 12, 1995, which told of the death of motor racing pioneer and Redlands native Louie Meyer.

Times sportswriter Shav Glick wrote:

> *When Louie Meyer died Saturday night at 91 in a Las Vegas hospital, it marked the end of a glorious era of American motor racing pioneers.*
>
> *Meyer, the Indianapolis 500s first three-time winner, was the last living winner of a pre–World War II Indy 500. He was also the last living builder of the famed Offenhauser engine that dominated open-wheel racing from 1947 into the mid-1970s. An Offy-powered car won every 500 from 1947 to 1964. Almost all were built in the Meyer-Drake garage in South-Central Los Angeles.*
>
> *Meyer was consumed with the sport. He worked on cars from the time he dropped out of school in Redlands in the eighth grade during a flu epidemic.*
>
> *"I went to work for my brother Eddie—he was 11 years older—as a mechanic in his garage during the epidemic and I never went back to school," Meyer said in a 1992 interview at his home in Searchlight, Nevada.*

Scholton told me that Louis Meyer's brother, Eddie, was almost a next-door neighbor when Scholton was a McKinley Elementary School student:

> *A next-door neighbor was anyone within ten acres of your citrus grove. My parents' home was almost on the southeast corner of Olive and San Mateo. The Meyer home was on the west side of San Mateo, approximately half way between Olive and Fern.*
>
> *Eddie Meyer's garage was on the south side of Redlands Boulevard, a half block west of First Interstate Bank.*

With children being literally few and far between, Scholton remembers that Eddie Meyer's son, though two or three years younger, was a playmate and fellow McKinley student. He says this memory covers the span of 1925–30, after which the Eddie Meyer family moved so that Eddie could help Louie Meyer in Los Angeles.

Scholton's reference to the citrus groves, which separated most Redlands houses in the first years of this century, is a reminder of the impact and influence the citrus industry had on the people living here then. Like other farming areas, the crop cycles were part of the rhythm of society, and the good and bad years were felt by all.

In talking to Redlands "long-timers" involved in growing oranges, I found several who said that some of their most vivid Christmas memories were of the years when celebrations had to be postponed due to freezing temperatures.

Navel oranges, Redlands' specialty crop, are especially vulnerable to cold weather. Navels are usually ready to pick around Christmastime, but they do not develop their full sugar content until sometime later. The lower the sugar content, the greater the impact of freezing temperatures.

Growers with low-lying groves hired smudging crews to light the oil burners set out through their groves. The crews were mostly made of grove workers seeking extra income, but many high school and college students were on standby for smudging crews. Later, wind machines and sprinkler systems were employed as alternatives, and in more recent times, helicopters have been brought in to act as gigantic fans to move the cold air up and bring warmer air down.

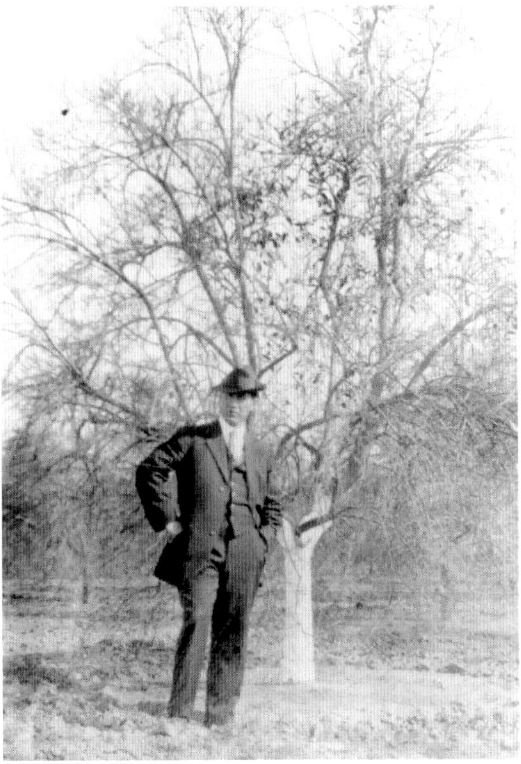

In 1913, the year of the Big Freeze, orange growers lost their crops and many trees. Normally leafy and green year round, this photo shows a grower surveying the damages.

The freeze of 1913 was the reality check that forced Redlands growers to rescind their belief that their valley was outside the frost belt. Since then, a cold night will still find farmers sleeping fitfully, waiting for the call that tells them that the temperature has dropped to the danger zone.

One friend of mine tells of the year she finally got her

act together to host a holiday party, only to have it canceled at the last minute because host and guests were out in the groves monitoring the temperature. Another time, she remembers taking her young daughter to the movies on Christmas Day, as a prolonged siege of cold weather delayed their family celebration for a whole week.

Still, unless you are an orange grower, it is hard to complain about the weather in Southern California.

Redlands Votes for Women

> *"And what are you going to do with the ballot when you get it?" the anti-suffragette demanded.*
>
> *"I am going to vote for the Good, the Beautiful and the True," the suffragette declared.*
>
> *"Oh, no you're not," the anti-suffragette flashed back. "They aren't going to be running."*

This anecdote is told by Frank E. Moore (quoting a story told by Redlands suffragette Eva Jahn) in his book *With a Grain of Salt.* August 1920 saw the passage of the Nineteenth Amendment to the United States Constitution. Fifty years after Susan B. Anthony first struck the blow for suffrage, and fourteen years after her death, female citizens throughout the country won the right to vote.

The women of Redlands had achieved this right nearly a decade earlier. A parallel movement to the national amendment push had spurred many states, primarily in the West, to make universal suffrage part of their original state constitutions. Wyoming (1890) and Utah (1897) came into statehood with suffrage for women in their constitutions. Washington, Idaho and Colorado followed.

The Redlands *Citrograph* was an early proponent of the measure. Mary Lynde Craig wrote a column in the 1890s entitled "The Women's Department." She chronicled the suffrage movement both from her vantage point in Northern California and from her family connections to Redlands. Wife of editor Scipio Craig, she was coeditor of the *Citrograph* and an attorney at law, practicing in San Francisco.

Craig kept her *Citrograph* readers up to date and did not hesitate to editorialize with her own opinions. Her disgust with politicians sounds strangely modern: "Congress adjourned last Tuesday and the whole country breathes easier." Full of hope, she wrote in the fall of 1894, "Ladies of Redlands should study the political platform in view of what is coming."

James H. Budd had been elected governor of the state of California. One of his campaign promises was to the cause of women's suffrage. Craig covered the inaugural proceedings in Sacramento and delivered a scathing report of Budd's selling out on this issue. In his entire address, not one word was made of voting rights for women. Suffrage was one of several amendment items on the 1895 ballot, but it was effectively killed by Budd's withdrawal of support.

Real action on the vote for suffrage would wait until Hiram Johnson's Republican gubernatorial victory of November 1910. The California legislature was swept with reform fever. A special statewide election was called for October 10, 1911, with suffrage number four of twenty-three proposed amendments covering a wide variety of reform measures.

Local organizations like the Contemporary Club declared that they "heartily supported the Susan B. Anthony amendment for equal suffrage." Redlands patroness Jennie Davis called for the creation of a Civic Improvement League within the club, so that they might take advantage of their soon-to-be-gained voting power. The Redlands Political Equality League went to work. Over a three-month period, they sent out 6,445 letters, held five rallies and distributed 7,000 leaflets.

On one occasion, the Wyatt Opera House was nearly filled with league supporters to listen to an address by Francis J. Heney, the great graft prosecutor. The address was supposed to be devoted to women's suffrage, but he hardly mentioned it, choosing instead to focus on corruption issues. The *Redlands Daily Facts* reported that Heney was visited behind the scenes afterward by the members of the Political Equality League and taken to task for the omission.

On October 9, the *Facts* recommended a yes vote on Amendment no. 4, women's suffrage. The October 10, 1911 issue reported a no-heavier-than-usual voter turnout:

> *No automobiles were seen scurrying about hurrying voters to the polls; no one was heard calling to friends across the street, asking whether they had voted. Occasionally one was heard to say "Did you vote for the women today?," but the answer reads both ways—both sides claimed to be voting for women.*

The opponents' favorite argument was that suffrage would impose a burden, a duty, an obligation, from which women were presently free.

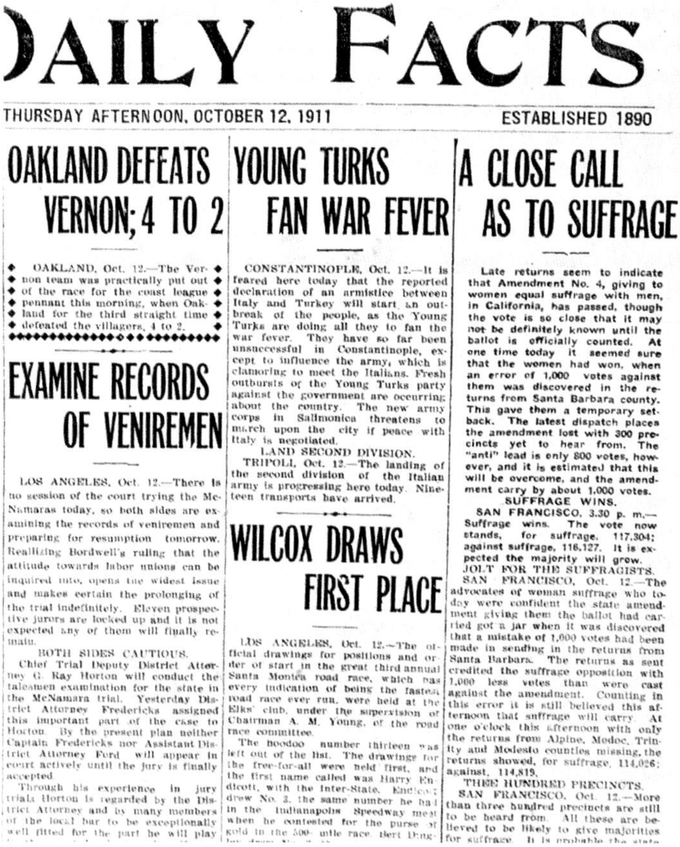

DAILY FACTS

THURSDAY AFTERNOON, OCTOBER 12, 1911 ESTABLISHED 1890

OAKLAND DEFEATS VERNON; 4 TO 2

OAKLAND, Oct. 12.—The Vernon team was practically put out of the race for the coast league pennant this morning, when Oakland for the third straight time defeated the villagers, 4 to 2.

EXAMINE RECORDS OF VENIREMEN

LOS ANGELES, Oct. 12.—There is no session of the court trying the McNamaras today, so both sides are examining the records of veniremen and preparing for resumption tomorrow. Realizing Bordwell's ruling that the attitude towards labor unions can be inquired into, opens the widest issue and makes certain the prolonging of the trial indefinitely. Eleven prospective jurors are locked up and it is not expected any of them will finally remain.

BOTH SIDES CAUTIOUS.

Chief Trial Deputy District Attorney G. Ray Horton will conduct the talesmen examination for the state in the McNamara trial. Yesterday District Attorney Fredericks assigned this important part of the case to Horton. By the present plan neither Captain Fredericks nor Assistant District Attorney Ford will appear in court actively until the jury is finally accepted.

Through his experience in jury trials Horton is regarded by the District Attorney and by many members of the local bar to be exceptionally well fitted for the part he will play

YOUNG TURKS FAN WAR FEVER

CONSTANTINOPLE, Oct. 12.—It is feared here today that the reported declaration of an armistice between Italy and Turkey will start an outbreak of the people, as the Young Turks are doing all they to fan the war fever. They have so far been unsuccessful in Constantinople, except to influence the army, which is clamoring to meet the Italians. Fresh outbursts of the Young Turks party against the government are occurring about the country. The new army corps in Salimonica threatens to march upon the city if peace with Italy is negotiated.

LAND SECOND DIVISION.

TRIPOLI, Oct. 12.—The landing of the second division of the Italian army is progressing here today. Nineteen transports have arrived.

WILCOX DRAWS FIRST PLACE

LOS ANGELES, Oct. 12.—The official drawings for positions and order of start in the great third annual Santa Monica road race, which has every indication of being the fastest road race ever run, were held at the Elks' club, under the supervision of Chairman A. M. Young, of the road race committee.

The hoodoo number thirteen was left out of the list. The drawings for the free-for-all were held first, and the first name called was Harry Endicott, with the Inter-State. Endicott drew No. 3, the same number he had in the Indianapolis Speedway meet when he contested for the purse of gold in the 500-mile race. Bert Ding-

A CLOSE CALL AS TO SUFFRAGE

Late returns seem to indicate that Amendment No. 4, giving to women equal suffrage with men, in California, has passed, though the vote is so close that it may not be definitely known until the ballot is officially counted. At one time today it seemed sure that the women had won, when an error of 1,000 votes against them was discovered in the returns from Santa Barbara county. This gave them a temporary setback. The latest dispatch places the amendment lost with 300 precincts yet to hear from. The "anti" lead is only 800 votes, however, and it is estimated that this will be overcome, and the amendment carry by about 1,000 votes.

SUFFRAGE WINS.

SAN FRANCISCO, 3.30 p. m.—Suffrage wins. The vote now stands, for suffrage, 117,304; against suffrage, 116,127. It is expected the majority will grow.

JOLT FOR THE SUFFRAGISTS.

SAN FRANCISCO, Oct. 12.—The advocates of woman suffrage who today were confident the state amendment giving them the ballot had carried got a jar when it was discovered that a mistake of 1,000 votes had been made in sending in the returns from Santa Barbara. The returns as sent credited the suffrage opposition with 1,000 less votes than were cast against the amendment. Counting in this error it is still believed this afternoon that suffrage will carry. At one o'clock this afternoon with only the returns from Alpine, Modoc, Trinity and Modesto counties missing, the returns showed, for suffrage, 114,026; against, 114,819.

THEE HUNDRED PRECINCTS.

SAN FRANCISCO, Oct. 12.—More than three hundred precincts are still to be heard from. All these are believed to be likely to give majorities for suffrage. It is probable the state

California women won the right to vote in 1911. It was a close race, with the outcome uncertain for days after the October 10 election.

The October 11 issue of the *Daily Facts* announced the defeat of Amendment no. 4. The vote tally was 85,126 for and 91,803 against. Editor Lyman M. King wrote, "The ladies will have to wait yet a little before they can vote in California." It was a sad day for the suffragists. However, the mood went the opposite direction the next day, when the papers reported a turnaround in the count. In the end, the victory margin was narrow throughout the state. Redlands passed the amendment by a majority of twenty-six votes. As Frank Moore wrote, "Nonetheless, a win is a win."

One hundred years later, I'd like to think that Eva Jahn's suffragette friend was on to something. We could all use a few more votes for the Good, the Beautiful and the True.

Part III
Keeping Busy in the Days Before Television

Don't tell the children, but without television, movies or YouTube, people actually managed to amuse themselves at the turn of the last century.

Redlands in 1900 was a town with an established year-round population that expanded each winter as wealthy "snowbirds" fled the icy cold of the Midwest and eastern states. A survey of the local papers, the *Redlands Daily Facts* and the *Citrograph* showed a marked increase in social reporting every year in October and November and a corresponding decrease in May and June.

Parties, fancy dress balls, musical performances and "at homes" were regularly reported and commented on. Church activities naturally increased during the Thanksgiving and Christmas holiday seasons. Social clubs and philanthropic organizations got their work done and had fun at the same time.

Then, as now, church denominations of all kinds were available for your choice of worship. The intersection of Cajon and Olive had become the "Lord's Corner" with the establishment of the First Baptist Church, the First Congregational Church (moved from its earlier location on Church Street) and the First Methodist Church. These churches still occupy the corner today. Trinity Episcopal Church was originally on the southeast corner. That building became a mortuary and then the home of the YWCA; today it is an office building.

The Redlands branch of the YMCA was organized in 1887. It was the first in Southern California and the second in the state to own its own building. The YMCA quickly assumed a leading place in the community. Its spacious building on the northwest corner of Cajon and Vine offered a cozy reading room with a fireplace and a place for chess players to challenge one another. Lectures and demonstrations of newfangled technology such as the Edison Talking Machine, or phonograph, were available.

In 1900, the Smiley Library was two years old. Residents could join the library by proving residency on the proper form and obtaining the signature of a resident taxpayer. Nonresidents had to pay fifty cents per month or one dollar per quarter as dues. Then, as now, books and periodicals for use in the reading room were free to all.

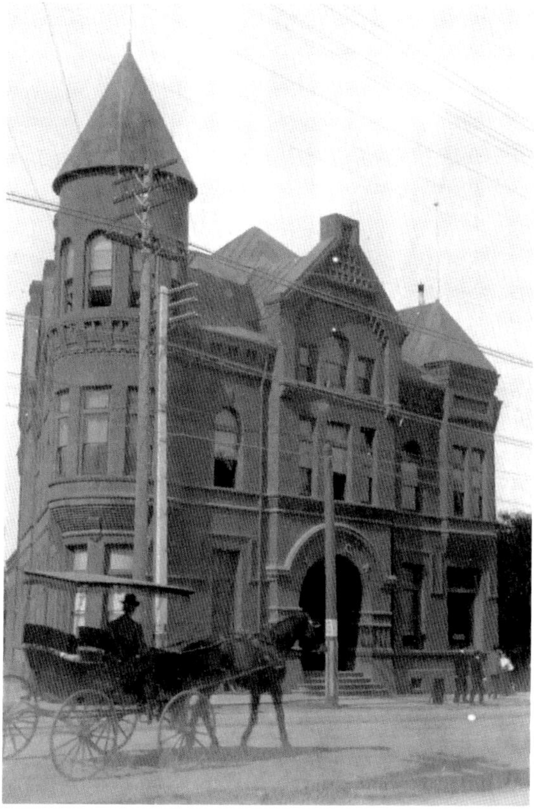

From 1892 to 1914, the YMCA occupied this imposing building on the northwest corner of Cajon and Vine.

In addition to social groups built around church congregations, many civic clubs were formed. Three are still active today: the Contemporary Club, the Fortnightly Club and The Spinet.

The Contemporary Club was the prominent women's club in the early part of the century. It brought speakers, assigned books to read and promoted intellectual development for women. Its clubhouse, a fanciful structure built in 1904, was across Vine Street from the YMCA. It featured meeting rooms and a large auditorium with mezzanine seating. The club moved to its present location on Eureka Street when the building was razed in 1971 to make way for a Vine Street widening project. Alas, no one bothered to notice ahead of time that the agreement governing the city's arrangement with Smiley Park forbid making any changes to Vine Street in the block west of the intersection of Vine and Eureka. A lovely building was lost.

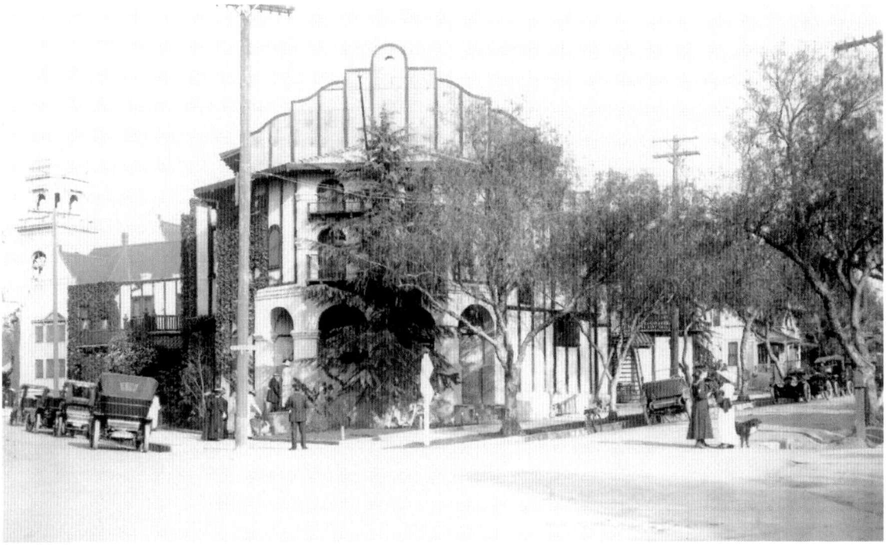

Organized in 1893 by twenty-five prominent women, the Redlands Contemporary Club is one of the oldest continuing community organizations in the country. This photo from 1913 features two girls conversing on the right. One of them wears a sailor-style blouse similar to the uniform worn by today's Kimberly Juniors.

A group of men formed the Fortnightly Club in 1895 to bring new arrivals together for a literary and social club. Meetings were held in members' homes. A key feature of this club is the requirement that each member do a research project periodically to present at a meeting. This has resulted in a rich collection of informative works on a variety of topics. The entire collection is catalogued at A.K. Smiley Public Library and available in the Heritage Room. In 1997, Dr. James Fallows began putting the papers on the club's website, making them available to all.

The Spinet was originally a piano club, but it soon broadened its focus and began organizing an annual concert series that brought the finest artists from around the world. A famous European musician of the era was quoted as saying, "I know three towns in America: New York, San Francisco, and Redlands." The cultural legacy of The Spinet is felt today through the efforts of the Redlands Community Music Association, which brings summer concerts and productions to the Redlands Bowl.

Many lodges and fraternal orders met regularly. Native Sons of the Golden West and the Women's Christian Temperance Union were active.

The city directory tells us that the Redlands Branch of the Woman's National Indian Association had a membership of sixty and met every six weeks at the homes of members: "The object of the association is twofold: To strengthen through the public press and through representatives at Washington, public sentiment with regard to justice for Indians; by our own educational and mission work among Indians to hasten their civilization, Christianization and enfranchisement."

The men and women of Redlands society did not believe in squandering their free time, and it was unusual for a middle- or upper-class woman to work for pay outside the home. Though women did not receive voting privileges in California until 1911 (1920 nationally), they found many opportunities in these volunteer organizations to make an impact on their community. This is a tradition that continues today.

Even at the Turn of the Century, Redlands Was Bicycle Crazy

> *Two handsome bicycles were being propelled by two tourists from somewhere last Saturday. Verily Redlands is putting on airs.*
>
> –Citrograph, *1888*

The bicycle made its appearance in the 1880s. Bicycling quickly became a popular pastime with both men and women. Once pneumatic (air-filled) tires appeared in 1891, bicycle riding jumped dramatically. Over 1 million bicycles were in use in the 1890s, and bicycle clubs sprang up all over the country.

In Redlands, the local cycling club purchased seven acres at Colton and Herald Streets. A grandstand overlooked a track enclosing a baseball and football field. Eight- to fifteen-foot-high fencing surrounded the facility. A fundraising gala to benefit the club and finance the fence was held at the Academy of Music. Titled "Spectacular and Operatic Carnival de Merchants," it was billed as the social event of the season. Historian L.E. Nelson neglected to give us the date, but his book, *Only One Redlands*, covers some of the highlights of the program:

> *The Boston Shoe Company came next in the person of Miss Nettie Hoskins, whose dress was covered with footwear of every description, with a good sized shoe upon her head and a bunch of strings hanging down her back…*
>
> *Miss Ethel Johnson made a unique display for F.A. Matthews. Her rich plush gown was bedecked with numerous household utensils, while from her shoulders a small awning was raised and lowered as she marched in review…*

The Newport Lumber Company furnished laths and shingles with which to trim the costume of Miss Mamie McIntosh…

Mrs. C.F. Rockwell chimed the music of the orchestra on an anvil from McLean's Blacksmith Shop…

The next appearance created prolonged mirth. Miss Mabel Farrer carried in one arm a live black pig and in the other a bunch of sausages, while singing "This little pig went to market," etc. The young porker was from J.S. Crosley's Meat Market.

First prize was won by the electric light company, with Mrs. T.J. Kennard in a pale blue costume, beneath which were a number of incandescent lights. She carried an electric torch and from her crown a myriad of colored lights sparkled. She was Liberty enlightening the world.

As women took up the sport of cycling, clothing customs altered accordingly. First, ladies were allowed to shorten their skirts several inches, but they sewed weights in the hems to keep leg-revealing flapping to a minimum. Amelia Bloomer, New York editor of *Lily*, a women's rights and temperance magazine, shocked the country in 1850 by appearing in public in trousers. Though Bloomer abandoned the outfit because of the derision it evoked, the Turkish-type pantaloons found acceptability as an exercise costume.

In 1895, the daring Mrs. Celia Cheeks introduced bloomers to the streets of Redlands. Mrs. Cheeks had been a waitress in Redlands until a career change led her to a job in sales for a Riverside cycling magazine.

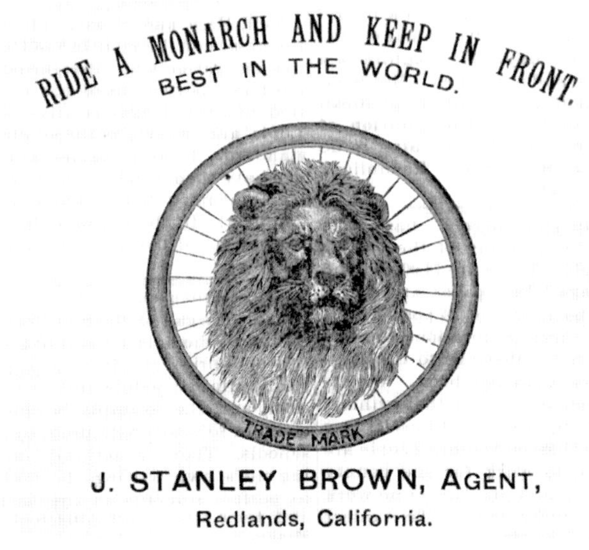

The Monarch Bicycle Company of Chicago often embellished its ads with a picture of Cupid pointing his bow at a couple cycling side by side. This ad is from the *Redlands Daily Facts*, circa 1895.

Though paved roads were scarce, long-distance racing was popular. Runs between Redlands and Bear Valley, Ensenada, Vacaville and San Francisco were not unknown. Nelson noted, "R.C. Sheperd and Elmer Morrow start…from Los Angeles for a bicycle race to this city…The winner takes both machines."

So popular was the two-wheeled form of transportation that the board of supervisors granted a right-of-way for a bicycle track from Redlands to San Bernardino. The track was three feet wide, graded and rolled though not paved. The course followed Colton Avenue west to Tippecanoe, turned north over the Tippecanoe bridge and on to the Cole race track in San Bernardino.

Almost as suddenly as it began, the bicycle craze ended. Cass Gaylord of Redlands took delivery on August 10, 1899, of the first automobiles west of the Rocky Mountains. Like children with a new app for their iPad, those with money and the leisure time to enjoy it abandoned their bicycles for the thrill of motorized vehicles.

Bicycles settled into the familiar role of providing mobility to the younger set. Several generations of boys, in particular, share memories of exploration, paper routes and general mischief thanks to their Schwinns or Montgomery Ward specials.

Frank Moore wrote a "With a Grain of Salt" column about boys who hitched a tow on other vehicles. It was against the law, but

> *when the streetcar made a slow right-angle turn, as when going from Cypress to Center, a kid on a bike could pump hard, catch up with the trolley and hang on. The grip was excellent because a horizontal grillwork of bars ran along the lower part of the windows and afforded a firm hold.*
>
> *Occasionally an exasperated motorman might stop his car at Palm to let out passengers and then bawl out the kids who had been hitching a free ride. But there was an understanding in boyland that bawlings out were part of life and not to be taken too seriously.*

Whether you ride or spectate, enjoy the Annual Redlands Bike Classic, established in 1985. Fundraisers for the event might consider a reprise of the "Spectacular and Operatic Carnival de Merchants."

After Bicycles, Cars Came to Redlands

For Sale—Used mules, four of them, model '04, parts all there. Come early and avoid their heels. Phone Suburban 9023 day time, Main 405 till bed time.

–Only One Redlands, *L.E. Nelson*

Redlands was the first town west of the Rockies to feet the impact of automotive history. Nelson's book carries an account of the arrival of Cass Gaylord's first automobile:

Automobiles were so new in America (the first one having been sold only four years earlier) that neither Gaylord nor the city council knew whether his was legal in Redlands. Gaylord, accordingly, asked for an ordinance permitting travel by automobile on the streets of the city, if such were thought necessary. The board was of opinion that the streets were open to such vehicles without further action, and Chairman Fowler expressed his willingness to give a permit if required.

Made in Kokomo, Indiana, Gaylord's $1,200 Haynes-Apperson arrived needing repairs, but on August 10, 1899, the *Redlands Daily Facts* reported that

the machine made its appearance…there was a general emptying of the business houses by the rush of the people to see the thing run. The Facts reporter was invited for a spin, and experienced the peculiar and pleasurable sensation of driving without the annoyance of the horse's switching its tail…

No horses broke from their moorings and there were no runaways. A crowd of boys followed…about the streets upon their wheels, as they would the band wagon in a circus parade.

The trouble was that the Haynes-Apperson couldn't make the grade up Cajon, and Gaylord soon traded up to a more powerful model.

The second car to appear in Redlands was Dr. Christopher Sanborn's Locomobile (shipped unassembled). The intrepid Dr. Sanborn drove his machine up the unpaved road we now know as Highway 18 and continued over to Big Bear and down the road through Mill Creek. Since this passage was challenging with a horse and wagon, Sanborn's trip must have been quite an adventure.

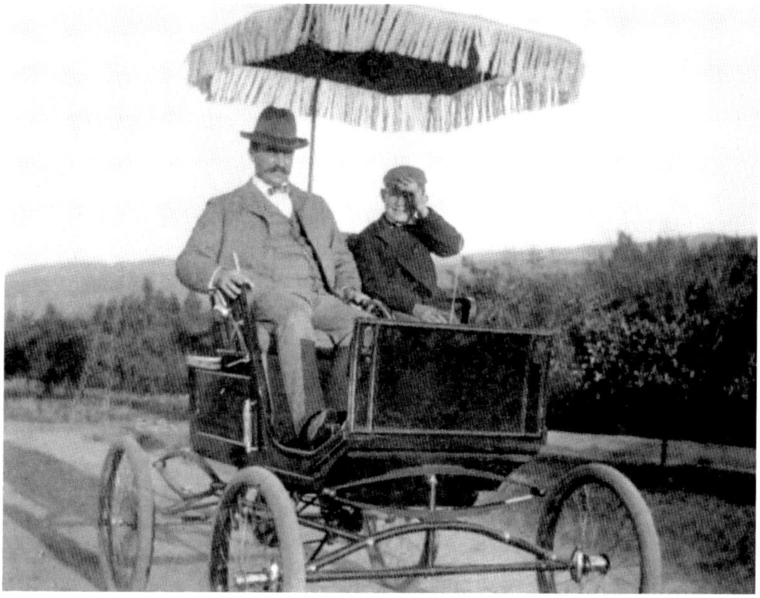

Dr. Christopher Sanborn paid $600 for this steam Locomobile in 1900. Despite its fragile appearance, the Locomobile was actually quite durable. Dr. Sanborn tested the vehicle around town and then invited his friend F.E. Olds of Los Angeles to join him for a trip up the City Creek lumber road past Fredalba to the Rim of the World road. Despite a deeply rutted dirt roadway and 25 percent grades, the little car safely made the round trip.

The third car in the city was a chain-driven one-cylinder Oldsmobile owned by Herman Furst. Furst taught many prominent Redlanders to drive. By 1909, there were 291 licensed autos in Redlands and nine car dealerships. Rivalry between brands was high. Redlanders could pay anything from $550 for a ten-horsepower Baby Reo to $5,000 for a fifty-five-horsepower Apperson Jack Rabbit.

Stock car racing and performance competitions were popular throughout Southern California. Never a town to be left out of doing the "in-thing," Redlands auto enthusiasts organized the Mile High Climb in 1909. William G. Moore's book *Redlands Yesterdays* describes this racing event. Automobiles were grouped in several classes plus a free-for-all. Well-known race driver Ralph Hamlin is shown surrounded by the crowd at the start of the race. Hamlin and his lookout, Guy K. Irwin, are waiting in their air-cooled Franklin named "Greyhound II." Since the route of the race was over one-lane roads, the lookout was necessary to keep an eye on the rear. If another car came within one hundred yards, the lookout's job was to warn the driver so that he could pull out and let the other pass.

Moore reported:

> *The race started in front of the Casa Loma Hotel on Orange at Colton, proceeded down Orange to Citrus, east on Citrus and diagonally to Fifth Avenue, Sand Canyon, on to Casa Blanca, the ranch of Leon Atwood on Oak Glen Road above Bryant, then to Oak Glen Lodge at an elevation of 4,920 feet.*
>
> *E.S. Seifert, driving a Stoddard-Dayton, won the free-for-all class in 24 minutes, 12 seconds, nosing out Ralph Hamlin by a minute and a half. The Hill Climb proved to be sensational with a large entry and crowds of spectators.*

For ordinary citizens, the shift from horse and buggy to automobile required changes in laws of the road. Redlands speed ordinance no. 322 forbade driving automobiles on the sidewalks. It also set a speed limit of twelve miles per hour and made it unlawful to pass any intersection or turn

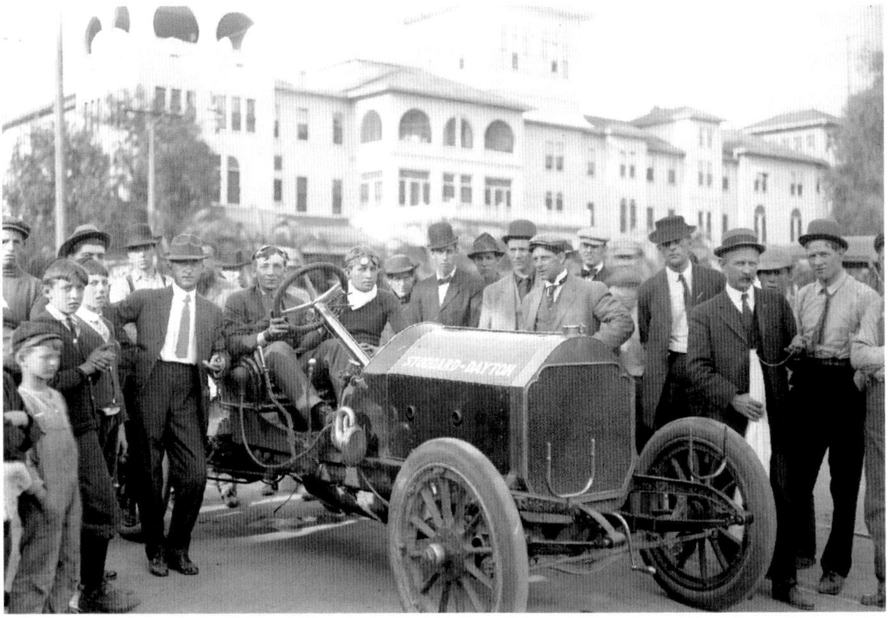

By 1909, there were 291 licensed cars in Redlands. Enthused motorists caught racing fever and organized a spectacular event. The Mile High Climb began at the Casa Loma Hotel on the corner of Orange and Colton in Redlands. The cars drove south on Orange, east onto Citrus and diagonally out to Fifth Avenue to Sand Canyon, where they climbed to 4,920 feet to the finish at the Oak Glen Lodge.

any corner faster than four miles an hour. Redlands also passed an ordinance limiting street parking to fifteen minutes, not because of a shortage of parking space but because the dripping of gasoline from the cars damaged the new asphalt pavement.

Then there was the question of propriety. Was it decent for women to be interested in automobiles? Nelson wrote:

> *A. Osbun, the agent of the Tourist automobiles in Redlands…wishes it thoroughly understood that ladies as well as gentlemen are invited* [to his auto show]. *A large number of ladies were in attendance Saturday, but some stayed away, not knowing whether it was the right place for them to go or not.*
>
> *Automobiling is becoming a fad with women, and not a few ladies are seen on the streets each day driving their own machines. In Redlands the majority are driving electrics, but a few of the more venturesome women are running the gasoline cars.*

This liberation, of course, could not come about without a bit of ridicule:

> *Mary had a motor car, propelled by gasoline,*
> *And everywhere that Mary went she rode in the machine.*
> *The motor struck a stone one day, and from its course deflected—*
> *Doctor says that Mary is as well as he expected.*

Still, a car is better than a mule.

Motorcycles Came to Town, Stayed

> *The motorcycle is little, but when it comes to making noise, it asks no odds of a boiler foundry. And such a noise it makes! Any horse other than a wooden one would feel like taking to the woods if it heard a motorcycle behind it. Fortunately the machines cost too much to become numerous.*
>
> –Redlands Daily Facts, *1902*

Alas, this prophecy never came to pass. Redlands developed motor fever and never looked back. Bicycles, the rage of the 1880s and '90s, along with fancy horses and their livery, coexisted with motor vehicles as long as they could, but they were no match for the lure of the new machines.

In 1901, Scipio Craig, the irrepressible, original booster of Redlands, proclaimed, "Can anyone see any good reason why Redlands would not be a good place for an automobile factory? Climactic conditions are far more favorable than in the east or north."

Nelson offered us a look at the enthusiastic way Redlands embraced the new technology:

> *Already Redlands minds were at work. O.H. Ensign invented a simple, compact automobile engine...Herman Furst built a small compact car to be used in parades...Sitwell and Johnson designed and constructed a car propelled by a rotary engine, small, noiseless, without vibration...H.M. Wright concocted a trick motorcycle guaranteed to break any speed law that was ever made.*

Of motorcycles, the *Facts* continued: "Bad as is the automobile, the motorcycle is worse. There was one of these machines in town yesterday, the agent having ridden it from Los Angeles, and by his own admission, you can trace the roads he traveled by the wrecks of vehicles he left behind him."

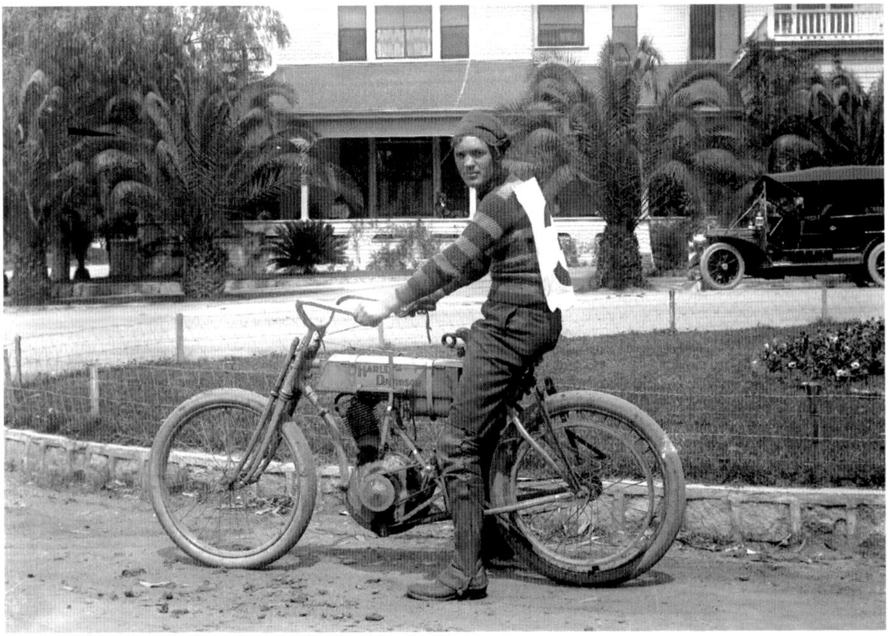

Motorcycle enthusiast Severn West poses in front of the Casa Loma Hotel in Redlands. He is ready for the motorcycle division of the Mile High Climb. Charles Gordon rode his Excelsior motorcycle to victory in 18.05 minutes.

The new aficionados soon formed a motorcycle club, and the 1909 Mile High Hill Race from Redlands to Oak Glen included a motorcycle division. The problem with motorcycles was the noise that they made. Automobiles managed to merge with the remaining population of horse-drawn buggies, but motorcycles made a racket that was beyond the tolerance of the average four-footed variety of transport.

Nelson quoted a motorcycle satire that appeared in 1910:

> *Motorcyclists to Be Restricted by Rules of Farmer Protective Society…*
>
> *The tillers of the soil met at Squire Bugg's house in Pumpkin Hollow and the farmers' Anti-Motorcycle Protective Society was formed. It is planned to meet weekly and draft such laws as may be necessary…Just now the rules read:*
>
> *(1) On discovering an approaching team, the motorcyclist must stop off-side and cover his machine with a tarpaulin painted to correspond with the surrounding scenery.*
>
> *(2) In case a motorcyclist makes a team run away, the penalty will be $50 the first mile, $100 for the second mile, $200 for the third mile and doubling until the said team stops, in addition to the usual damage.*
>
> *(3) The speed limit on country roads this year will be secret and the penalty for violation will be $10 for every mile caught going in excess of said limit.*
>
> *(4) On approaching a corner where he cannot command a view of the road ahead, the motorcyclist must dismount not less than a hundred yards from the turn, toot his horn, ring the bell, fire off a revolver, and send up three bombs at intervals of five minutes.*
>
> *(5) Motorcycles must again be seasonable painted. They must be green in spring, golden in summer, red in autumn and orange color in winter.*
>
> *(6) Motorcyclists running on the country roads at night must send up a red rocket every mile, and wait ten minutes for the road to clear. They may then proceed carefully, blowing their horns and shooting sky rockets.*
>
> *(7) In case a horse will not pass a motorcycle, notwithstanding the scenic tarpaulin, the motorcyclist must take the machine apart as rapidly as possible, conceal the parts about his person and walk down the road.*

Of course, none of this deterred the growing popularity of the motorcycle. Stories are told of the Putnam Brothers' grocery store on Stillman Avenue near the University of Redlands. Clyde Putnam and his cousin used to deliver groceries on motorcycles.

Clyde became famous for the enormous loads he could carry on his old Excelsior belt drive model. For amusement, he rode in parades or horrified his mother by dashing down the street backward or standing up on the seat. One of his favorite stunts was to ride up and down the stairway at the old Franklin school.

I don't know about you, but stuck in rush-hour traffic on one of our local freeways, I have sometimes wished for a special law for motorcycles. Maybe no. 3 in the previous list could be adapted for use today.

Redlands Was Once Considered a Sportsman's Paradise

> *With a surge of joy the boy rode his bicycle out of the high-school grounds. He did not hate the school, but to him it was like a term in some friendly prison. Something to be endured. For the rest of the daylight hours he was free to hunt over the brush-covered hills and green creek beds, frequented by cottontails, doves and quail…As he rode home through the twilight he wondered if other boys had as much fun as he did. They could not understand why he did not join in their games, and he could not understand their enjoyment of organized sport.*
>
> *–Franklin W. Nordhoff*

Thus begins the essay "After School," from the book *Fruit of the Earth*, published in 1955. This collection of essays written by Franklin Nordhoff (Redlands High School class of 1913) might not have found its way, along with his diaries, into the collection of the Heritage Room at the A.K. Smiley Public Library without Franklin's relationship to two other Nordhoffs.

Reading about the Nordhoff family leads me to wonder if there is a genetic component to wanderlust. Franklin's grandfather, Charles Nordhoff, the respected travel writer and New York editor, ran away to sea at the age of fourteen. Franklin's brother, Charley, the novelist best known for coauthoring *Mutiny on the Bounty*, traveled the world and settled in exotic Tahiti. The entire clan seems to have shared the attitude that life was an adventure waiting to happen.

Walter Nordhoff, son of Charles and father of Charley and Franklin, built a home in Redlands in 1899 and brought his wife and three youngest children—

Margaret, Franklin and Mary—to live here. Charley was off at boarding school but spent many school vacations exploring the Redlands area. Franklin was four years old when the family moved to Redlands. I use the verb "move" loosely because the Nordhoffs traveled freely and frequently between homes in Baja California, San Diego and Terminal Island (Los Angeles).

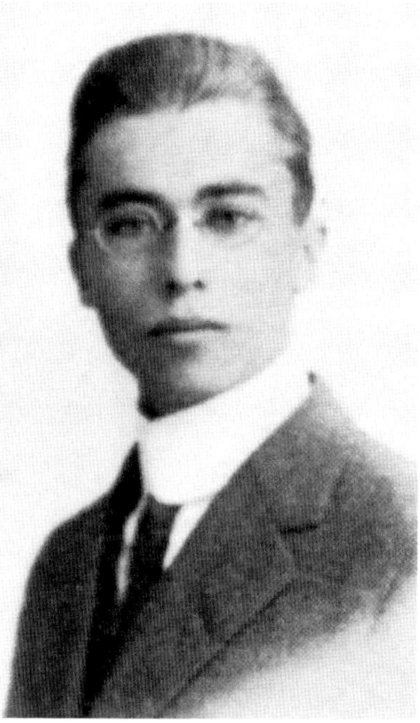

Franklin W. Nordhoff's photo in his 1913 yearbook, the *Makio*, is accompanied by this caption: "'Nitro'—Physics shark; has a mania for hunting. *Anticipation*: Mr. Nordhoff should be a science teacher who spends his vacations finding new specimens for which he invents new names. *Realization*: The magazine reading world will be thrilled by his vivid and realistic accounts relating his experiences while tracking rabbits in the Wash."

Fruit of the Earth and the set of Nordhoff diaries housed in the A.K. Smiley Public Library's Heritage Room are wonderful accounts and observations of times gone by. All of the Nordhoff children were sent to prominent boarding schools; Franklin did a stint at Choate, a private boarding school in Connecticut. I could find no stated reason for his return to school in Redlands; maybe it was his obvious love of the hunting and fishing opportunities to be found here.

The diary entries from Franklin's senior year of high school make little reference to school. He mentioned that he and his friend Leslie Gay attended the senior class play and groaned about a Saturday wasted writing a research paper. There is no mention of his participation in graduation ceremonies, and the writings are suggestive of a young man who views school as one of those formalities of life—something to be suffered through but not savored.

In the early part of the twentieth century, wild game was very plentiful in Southern California. A friend and frequent hunting partner of both Franklin and his brother Charley was Dr. Walter Power. Dr. Power, a well-known local physician, was also an avid huntsman. Power's son, Stuart Power, told me that his dad used to talk about the days when you could hunt antelope and dove in the Hemet Valley. The flocks of birds were so large and dense that they blocked out the sun.

Franklin Nordhoff's diaries tell of his wanderings around California. He would head off alone on his motorcycle, affectionately named the "Sand Crab," or with others in the family's automobile, which he affectionately named "Otto." Roads, when they existed at all, were primitive, and one was expected to be one's own mechanic much of the time. Some highlights of Nordhoff's adventures in 1913 follow:

> *April 5. Clear, warm, calm—Mill Creek—I got up at 3:15 and left at 4:15 on the Sand Crab. Rode up through Mentone, by the new road past the 2nd power house and on up the canyon. The Crab pulling like a twin this morning. Had easy going until after the 2nd ford, and from there on I had to get down and hump along, using the free wheel considerably…got within about three miles of Forest Home…Left my machine at 6:15…walked…*
>
> *May 9—Went up to Banning and saw the play…Margaret* [sister] *and some of the Redlands girls did a Roman Dance. Got home at 2 o'clock a.m. Otto ran extremely well, and we did the 26 miles in about an hour… Overhauled and varnished the Sand Crab on Saturday.*
>
> *May 24—Got up at 4 and got breakfast, pumped up tires, and filled gas tank on Sand Crab. Left the house at 5. Rode up to Beaumont and over Lamb's Canyon, through San Jacinto, Lakeview, Perris, Elsinore, Corona, Arlington, Riverside, and back to Redlands. 113 miles altogether. Got back at 11 o'clock…Peg (Margaret) came back from a 12 day visit in L.A…Later went down town and back (4 miles), up to the Country Club, down town and back (14 miles), and then Charley and I went* [to Riverside] *(30 miles). So 113+4+14+30 equals 161 miles on Saturday. Saw lots of rabbits.*
>
> *June 16, 17—Warm, clear, calm, full moon. Bear Valley—Lez Gay and I left the house (in Redlands) at 3:30 and went up by Santa Ana. Did not boil all the way up and made most of the Clark's on intermediate, although the Bear Creek Hill was low work after the bad mud hole. Pulled into the Pine Knot Store at 7:10, three hours and forty minutes for the run…Went back by the Crest Road, which has some terrific grades, on two of which the gasoline would not feed, so we had to jack up the rear end to fill the carburetor.*

Franklin W. Nordhoff Jr. introduced his father's diaries and summed up the feeling they convey: "The machines and roads of the time seem primitive now, but some of us would change our new cars and bulging freeways for an age with little traffic and open countryside, to see things as he did on the Sand Crab and in the family's Otto."

The Year Redlands Got the Flu, Everyone Got It

That the Spanish Influenza epidemic in Redlands is not of a serious nature and that closing of schools, churches or theaters at this time appears entirely unnecessary, was the consensus of opinion at a conference yesterday of Mayor Brock with the City Board of Health and the School Trustees. There are few cases in the city and in most of these cases the disease appears no more severe than grippe of recent years.

–Redlands Review, *October 13, 1918*

Within ten days of this optimistic statement, Mayor Brock, plus the city clerk, engineer, janitor and fire chief, were all flat on their backs with the flu. The flu epidemic of 1918–19 was the worst in modern history. Actually pandemic (worldwide) in nature, Spanish influenza appeared in Europe in the spring of 1918 and spread rapidly through the various forces fighting in the trenches of World War I. By the time the epidemic was over, more than 20 million people had died worldwide. In the United States, more than 500,000 died—far more than the number killed in the war.

Curious to know of the flu's impact on Redlands, I read through the daily (except Monday) issues of the *Redlands Review* of 1918. Influenza news began to appear regularly in late September. Within a few days, the reports were that well over 100,000 men in the army camps had been ill. The death toll was more than 2,500 and increasing by 650 every twenty-four hours.

Understandably, a bit of panic began to build. An editorial discussed the speculation that the German kaiser had fomented the disease as a war tactic. Though the papers took pains to discard this fear, rumors abounded.

By October 15, there had been seven deaths from flu in San Bernardino County. The city of San Bernardino declared that "[e]very physician in the city is working night and day and even at this are unable to take care of all the cases at hand, while the hospitals are filled to overflowing and every nurse obtainable has been placed in service. The Patton hospital had been quarantined, and the dinner planned for Governor Stephens this Tuesday evening will not be held."

On the same day, Redlands ordered all schools, churches, movie theaters, pool halls and cigar stores closed. Business hours were restricted, and public meetings were forbidden. Children were instructed to remain inside with their families. Chief of Police Larmore was instructed to enforce the order. Any gatherings that were too important to be canceled would not allow

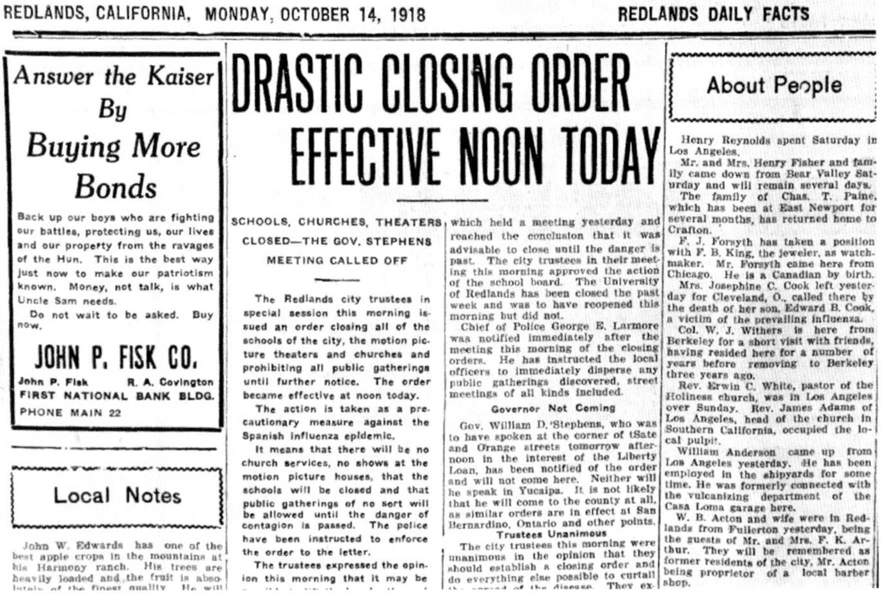

REDLANDS, CALIFORNIA, MONDAY, OCTOBER 14, 1918 REDLANDS DAILY FACTS

Answer the Kaiser By Buying More Bonds

Back up our boys who are fighting our battles, protecting us, our lives and our property from the ravages of the Hun. This is the best way just now to make our patriotism known. Money, not talk, is what Uncle Sam needs.

Do not wait to be asked. Buy now.

JOHN P. FISK CO.

John P. Fisk R. A. Covington
FIRST NATIONAL BANK BLDG.
PHONE MAIN 22

Local Notes

John W. Edwards has one of the best apple crops in the mountains at his Harmony ranch. His trees are heavily loaded and the fruit is abso-

DRASTIC CLOSING ORDER EFFECTIVE NOON TODAY

SCHOOLS, CHURCHES, THEATERS CLOSED—THE GOV. STEPHENS MEETING CALLED OFF

The Redlands city trustees in special session this morning issued an order closing all of the schools of the city, the motion picture theaters and churches and prohibiting all public gatherings until further notice. The order became effective at noon today.

The action is taken as a precautionary measure against the Spanish influenza epidemic.

It means that there will be no church services, no shows at the motion picture houses, that the schools will be closed and that public gatherings of no sort will be allowed until the danger of contagion is passed. The police have been instructed to enforce the order to the letter.

The trustees expressed the opinion this morning that it may be

which held a meeting yesterday and reached the conclusion that it was advisable to close until the danger is past. The city trustees in their meeting this morning approved the action of the school board. The University of Redlands has been closed the past week and was to have reopened this morning but did not.

Chief of Police George E. Larmore was notified immediately after the meeting this morning of the closing orders. He has instructed the local officers to immediately disperse any public gatherings discovered, street meetings of all kinds included.

Governor Not Coming

Gov. William D. Stephens, who was to have spoken at the corner of tSate and Orange streets tomorrow afternoon in the interest of the Liberty Loan, has been notified of the order and will not come here. Neither will he speak in Yucaipa. It is not likely that he will come to the county at all, as similar orders are in effect at San Bernardino, Ontario and other points.

Trustees Unanimous

The city trustees this morning were unanimous in the opinion that they should establish a closing order and do everything else possible to curtail

About People

Henry Reynolds spent Saturday in Los Angeles.

Mr. and Mrs. Henry Fisher and family came down from Bear Valley Saturday and will remain several days.

The family of Chas. T. Paine, which has been at East Newport for several months, has returned home to Crafton.

F. J. Forsyth has taken a position with F. B. King, the jeweler, as watchmaker. Mr. Forsyth came here from Chicago. He is a Canadian by birth.

Mrs. Josephine C. Cook left yesterday for Cleveland, O., called there by the death of her son, Edward B. Cook, a victim of the prevailing influenza.

Col. W. J. Withers is here from Berkeley for a short visit with friends, having resided here for a number of years before removing to Berkeley three years ago.

Rev. Erwin C. White, pastor of the Holiness church, was in Los Angeles over Sunday. Rev. James Adams of Los Angeles, head of the church in Southern California, occupied the local pulpit.

William Anderson came up from Los Angeles yesterday. He has been employed in the shipyards for some time. He was formerly connected with the vulcanizing department of the Casa Loma garage here.

W. B. Acton and wife were in Redlands from Fullerton yesterday, being the guests of Mr. and Mrs. F. K. Arthur. They will be remembered as former residents of the city, Mr. Acton being proprietor of a local barber shop.

On Monday, October 14, 1918, the *Redlands Daily Facts* announced that all public buildings were closed and events were cancelled do to the outbreak of Spanish influenza. Governor William Stephens's outdoor speeches on behalf of liberty bonds for support of America's involvement in World War I were included in the cancellations.

admittance to anyone unless they were wearing a gauze mask. Many wore one whenever they went out. Sad stories abounded. Whole families were stricken at once. Unable to get word to someone for help, the delirious would lay next to the dead for days. A special hospital for influenza patients was opened in Riverside. Two nurses, both in their early twenties, "gave their lives" to pneumonia following influenza.

The year 1918 was a tumultuous one. World War I was building to a climax in Europe. The women's suffrage movement was in full battle dress, skirmishing toward its 1920 national victory. In Redlands, the big political controversy surrounded the issue of prohibition, and the *Review* was elated when President Wilson signed the Wartime Prohibition Act to ban the manufacture or sale of liquor except for export.

Halloween was a quiet one in 1918. All stores and businesses had to be closed by six o'clock in the evening; no parties or trick-or-treating were allowed. An editorial noted the bright side: "[N]o need for general cleanup of debris, searching for gates and missing wagons and all those little affairs that occupy the public mind every first of November."

The University of Redlands was closed twice—once when the men's dorm housing the Student Army Training Corps was quarantined for the flu, and again when the illness swept the women's dorm. Football games, already reduced due to the shortage of male students, were postponed indefinitely. The schools were allowed to reopen on November 4, but attendance was five hundred below normal. Two days later, Mayor Brock lifted the ban on all but movie theaters, cigar stores and pool halls.

By the end of December, things were pretty much back to normal. Of the two thousand cases reported in Redlands, nineteen had resulted in deaths, usually from pneumonia. Harder hit, San Bernardino and Riverside suffered a 10 percent death rate among those with the disease. Hopefully, the identification of the influenza virus combined with the development of antibiotics and flu vaccines will make major flu epidemics something found only in history books.

For now, I do get my flu shots.

A Look at Redlands Movie History through the Peephole

> *For seven years Redlands dreamed of becoming a film producing center. An Essanay company arrived in 1911 to shoot westerns in the wash, in orange groves, in a studio on Lugonia two blocks west of Orange, using Indians from Banning, Cowboys from Arizona, New Mexico and Wyoming…*
>
> *Fox utilized the Grigsby home on West Cypress, and Redlands' bowling alley, sheriff's, Wells Fargo and Real Estate offices for a southern spectacular. Vitagraph took sleds and "Esquimaux" dogs to Bear Valley.*
>
> –*L.E. Nelson,* Only One Redlands

As Southern California developed an identity of its own, the 1900s saw a big change in the average person's leisure time. The workweek dropped from sixty-six hours in 1850 to fifty-six hours in 1900 and then fell to forty-one hours by 1920. Pianos and phonographs were available to the masses, and the record industry helped change musical tastes with songs such as "You Can Go as Far as You Like With Me in My Merry Oldsmobile."

Thomas Edison's invention of the kinetoscope, a machine that allowed viewers to watch moving pictures through a peephole, launched the movie industry. For a while, Edison resisted suggestions that films be projected on a screen. He feared a loss of profits if a mass of people viewed a film at the same time.

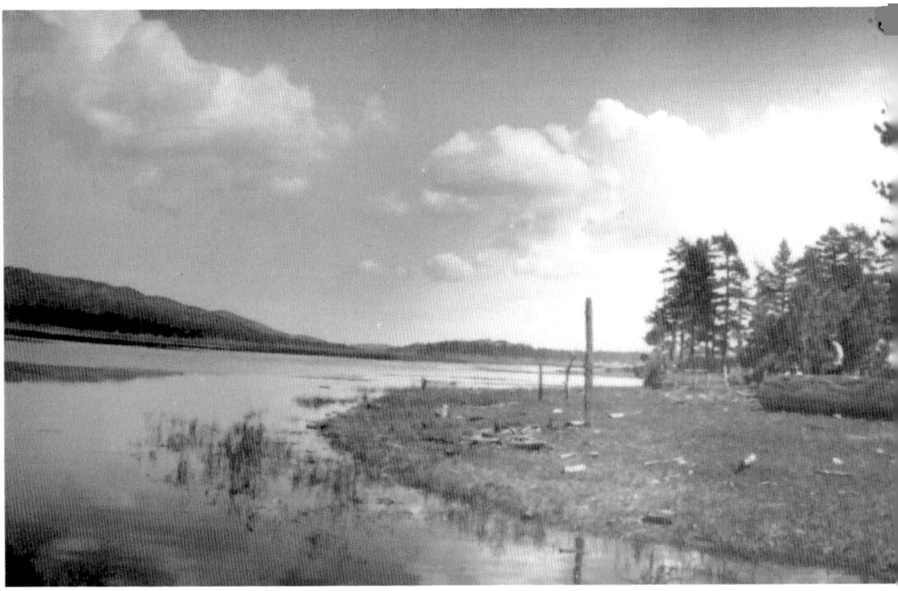

The Henry Fisher property at Big Bear Lake was the location for Cecile B. DeMille's film *The Call of the North*. Henry's son, John "Fritz" Fisher, later became DeMille's business manager. Fritz Fisher and friend Steward Edward Wright played Indians in the film. Wright was the author of the novel *Conjuror's House*, on which the film was based.

The first movie with a plot, *The Great Train Robbery* (1903), produced the first movie star, Max Aaronson. Also known as Bronco Billy Anderson, he is said to have had a lot at the northwest corner of Lugonia and Orange that he used for filming westerns.

This information comes from Frank Moore's column titled "Shades of Hollywood." Moore reported on an exchange he had with Cecil Sparks, who had been an extra on some of the films shot in Redlands. The area around Bear Valley proved to be popular with film companies that desired to shoot western themes in unspoiled settings. Since the closest lodging of any size was Redlands, it was natural that the companies would take notice of the local opportunities. The lighting was more dependable than fog-prone Los Angeles, and a company director interested in establishing a permanent location in Redlands glowingly noted, "We were in Smiley Heights this afternoon. Say, man, you could put on an eight-reel picture in that one place alone and get all the scenery you would need for it."

More than one company set up shop in Redlands. Most of the films were short, low-budget pieces. Director Julius Frankenberg formed a company titled Redlands Beauty Films, used the "R" on the mountains in its trademark

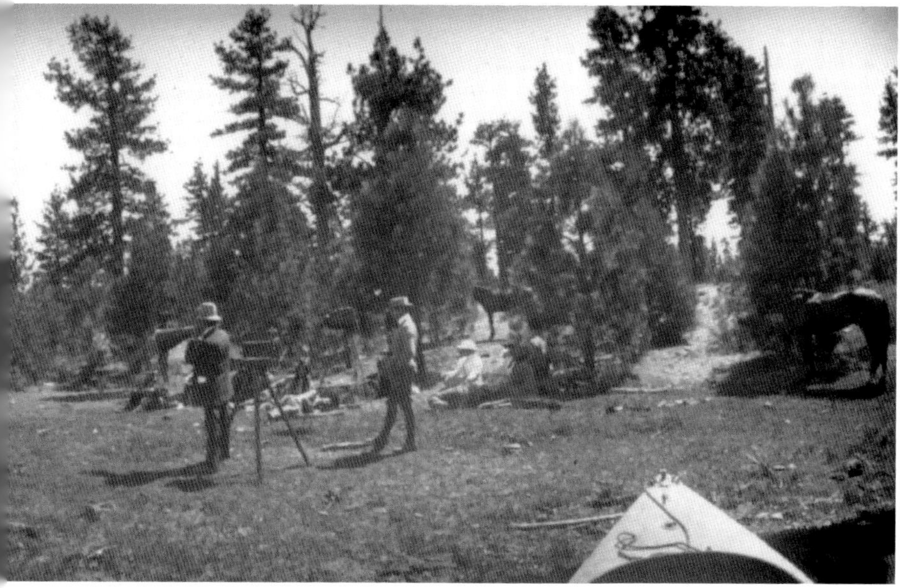

and hired C.E. Hubach, dean of music at the University of Redlands, to be its treasurer. Frankenberg produced a series called *The Adventures of Pietro*. One episode was filmed entirely in Henry Fisher's home and garden on Highland Avenue. Frankenberg not only directed but also played the parts of Pietro, Napoleon, Kaiser Wilhelm, King George and the sultan of Turkey. The plot seems to have been a kind of "Forrest Gump" tale, which would have Pietro bringing world rulers together to end World War I. An episode was also shot at Kimberly Crest.

In the flurry of interest that followed, Nelson told us:

> *The Fujiyama Feature Film Company negotiated for a Redlands studio and cooperation with Beauty Films. Other companies scouted studio sites. A film magazine sent staff writers.*
>
> *On the verge of motion picture history, the dream of movie affluence left Redlands quickly on the heels of an April 23, 1918, news note:*
>
> *"Miss Edith Hollister purchased for $30 three negative films of the Redlands Beauty Film Company to secure payment of a promissory note of $2,170..."*
>
> *Never again did Redlands mistake itself for Hollywood.*

One Redlander moved on to become part of the Hollywood scene. Henry Fisher's son, John (Fritz), allowed Cecil B. DeMille to use the Fisher's Big Bear property for the filming of *The Call of the North* in 1912. Five years later, Fritz Fisher's friendship with DeMille led to a job as DeMille's personal business manager and a career as financial advisor to the stars. William Moore's book *Fun with Fritz* is full of Fisher's photographs and memoirs of the early days of filmmaking.

What would Edison think of today's multiscreen theater complexes? I'm just happy I don't have to watch movies through a peephole.

Mulvihills Played with Skill and Class

The visit of an all-black baseball team from Los Angeles in the summer of 1910 inspired Harry and Arthur Beal to form Redlands' first African American baseball team.

In 1910, baseball was truly a national pastime. Football and basketball had been invented, but they did not have the popularity of baseball. Rugby and American football supporters were fighting for dominance for their respective sport, and the outcome was by no means certain.

Professional and semipro baseball leagues were closed to African American players. A decade later, official leagues of all-black teams were formed. In 1910, it was difficult, but possible, for African American athletes to make a living or supplement their incomes with their sport. Most towns and cities across the country had local teams, both white and black, who formed loose associations and played one another. Fans were charged for admission to the games. The proceeds covered the team's expenses and often provided bonus income for players.

In Redlands, several active white teams played successfully against one another and against teams from surrounding cities. What is known about this aspect of Redlands' history is found in the archives of the A.K. Smiley Public Library's collection of past issues of the *Redlands Daily Facts*. No oral history or photographs seem to have been handed down.

The first African American baseball team to play in Redlands was a Los Angeles team whose visit was arranged by Reverend Hubbard. The director of the YMCA, R.L. Glover, responded to the challenge and promised to organize a crack team of white Redlands ball players to play on July 4, 1910.

The *Facts* was an enthusiastic supporter of the game, no matter who played it, and carried almost daily coverage of both teams' player recruitment and lineup changes. The Los Angeles Giants was a conglomeration of players from three outstanding African American ball teams. These players had beaten most of the better white and African American teams in the West.

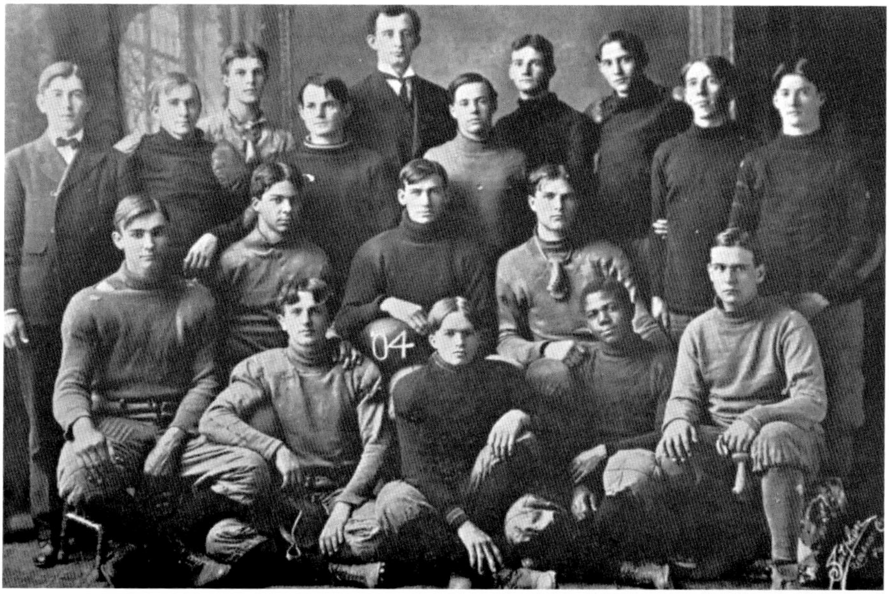

Charles Arthur Beal, identified in the *Makio* as Arthur Beal, was a member of the Redlands class of 1904. This photograph shows Arthur with the 1903 Redlands High School football team. He was also a member of the track team. Though he does not appear on the roster for the high school baseball team, Arthur was obviously a talented athlete.

Glover had some difficulty assembling a team and finally resorted to recruiting a couple of players from the Sherman Indian Institute—there evidently not being the same restrictions on Indian athletes as on African American ones. On July 4, 1910, the *Facts* reported that a crowd of several hundred turned out to watch the game, but no mention was made of the locally embarrassing outcome. That the YMCA team received a major drubbing from the Los Angeles Giants was only alluded to in future articles.

The outstanding performance of the Giants players must have inspired local African Americans. By July 27, 1910, the *Facts* reported that local black athletes had successfully formed their own team:

> *Ever since the colored baseball team, the Los Angeles Giants, played in Redlands on July 4, the colored men and boys of Redlands have been trying to organize a baseball team composed exclusively of their race. They have held several meetings, practiced a few times and are now fully organized… The aggregation has ordered suits through Mulvihill Bros., and have taken the name of Mulvihills. The suits are dark blue and the letters "Mulvihill" are in white across the front.*

Mulvihill was the name of a local emporium that sold sporting equipment. The first game was played several days later. Harry Beal had been named manager, and his brother, Arthur, was touted as "one of the fastest players in the game." The recruitment of some players from the Los Angeles Giants added to the lineup. A former Giants player named Brock was pitcher, and another, Joe Pryor, joined the team midseason as shortstop and heavy hitter. All in all, the team was a sensation, drawing large crowds to each game.

A game against the Arlingtons of Riverside played at the Redlands High School diamond proved especially entertaining for the fans. The *Facts* gushed: "The recent swatfest in Chicago when New York defeated the Cubs by a score of 18 to 9, forty-two hits being made by both teams, was a trivial incident compared with the slugging that was witnessed Saturday afternoon on the local diamond. The score of 14 to 11 nearly tells the tale."

A brawl erupted when the Arlington fans began disputing the umpire's calls. The Redlands fans rallied to support the local team, however, and the fight was averted.

The team was so successful that a Los Angeles promoter, the Spalding Agency, arranged for the Mulvihills to play a top-rated team from Los Angeles, the Boynton Bears. The Bears were a white team, with two brothers named DiMaggio (no known relation to Joe and Dom, but strong players, nonetheless). Games arranged by Spalding were highly coveted because they guaranteed that the teams would show up to play as scheduled.

The game against the Boynton Bears was to be played on Friday, September 9, California Admission Day. Even in 1910, state admission to the United States must have become an accepted state of affairs, as no other events were scheduled to commemorate the occasion. The *Facts* hyped the game with frequent stories leading up to the big date. Two days before the game, the tension was raised by the absence of Joe Pryor, who was called to Los Angeles because his mother was ill.

Pryor stepped off the train on the morning of the game, much to everyone's relief. The Boynton Bears also arrived in the morning, took a tour of Smiley Heights and then checked into their hotel. Everyone was on the field and ready to play by 2:00 p.m.

Unfortunately, the Mulvihills were no match for the experienced Los Angeles team. They lost, 21–6. The large crowd was behind the local team, and the *Facts* reported that it was a "good contest, anyway." The wind out of their sails, the Mulvihills lost their next few games. Finally, on September 19, they defeated the Indian baseball team of San Jacinto. There was again a large crowd, as a fiesta was underway on the Indian reservation. The *Facts*

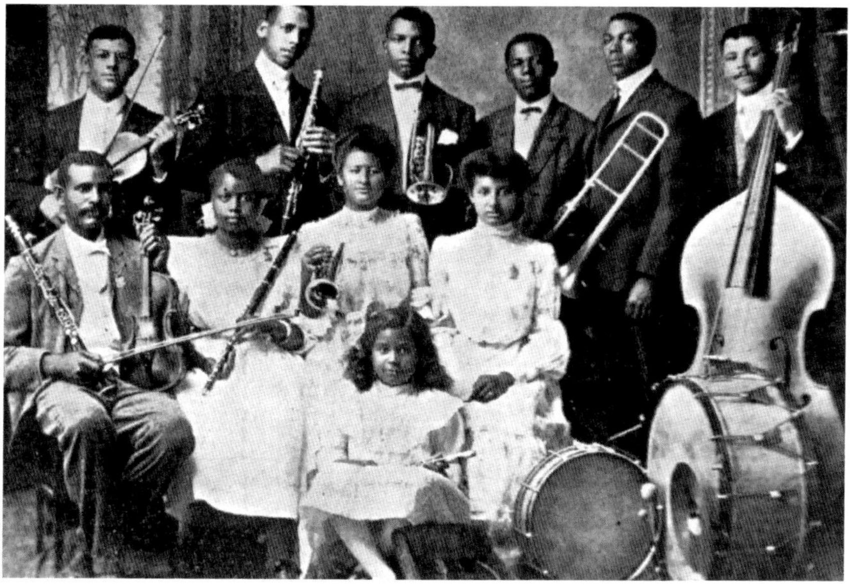

Charles Arthur Beal and his brother, Harry (fourth and fifth from left, top), were members of the Harbert family orchestra. They were sons of Martha Embers Beal and Israel Beal, who arrived in the valley in the 1850s and 1860s, respectively.

reported, "They took the tally-ho and on the return got lost…and did not find their way back until 6 o'clock this morning."

The team re-formed briefly the next season but soon evolved into an aggregation of black players from several Inland Empire teams, changing its name to the Brock All-Stars. Those listed on the team who played against the Boynton Bears were Brock, pitcher; Harbert, catcher; Harry Beal, first base; Carter, second base; Joe Pryor, shortstop; Harris, third base; Cooper, left field; Bush, center field; and Arthur Beal, right field.

Harry Beal owned a successful stage and car service transporting tourists up and down the local mountains. Arthur graduated from Redlands High School in 1905. Arthur was on the football and track teams at RHS, but his name is not on the baseball roster. Both were also musicians, and they are included with a photo of the Harbert family orchestra published in the *Colored Citizen*, an early Redlands newspaper now in the collection of the A.K. Smiley Public Library. Arthur later married Mabel Harbert.

Arthur is fondly remembered by many Redlanders as the first African American mail carrier in town, a helpful man who served in that post for a long career.

One can only wonder how many major-league baseball careers would have been possible if the Mulvihill players had been born a century later.

Part IV
Millionaires Brought Changes to the Town

Redlands is the richest town in the world, per capita.
—Citrograph, *February 8, 1902*

Before the 90210 zip code for Beverly Hills, California, became synonymous with wealth and high living, there was Redlands. Before Palm Springs became the winter playground of the rich, there was Redlands. One writer in Buffalo, New York, noted, "The man who likes to divide his time between looking leisurely at gorgeous surroundings and harassing a golf ball would be in his element in Redlands."

Early arrivals shared their discovery of the town with their many acquaintances in the East, causing others to direct their private railway cars (as many as thirty to forty were parked here some winters) west, with Redlands as the destination. These were not languishing playboy types, however. These millionaires turned their energy from building fortunes to building a town.

Among the earliest arrivals were identical twins Albert and Alfred Smiley, who purchased more than two hundred acres on the southern hills above town and built their winter homes. While not in the millionaire category, these Quaker gentlemen, at the time in their sixties, set the philanthropic tone for their new city that continues today. The first thing they did was to transform their properties into a botanical wonderland complete with lakes and miles of scenic drive. Then they invited the public to enjoy it free of charge. Cañon Crest Park, later known as Smiley Heights, became one of the most famous destinations in the world.

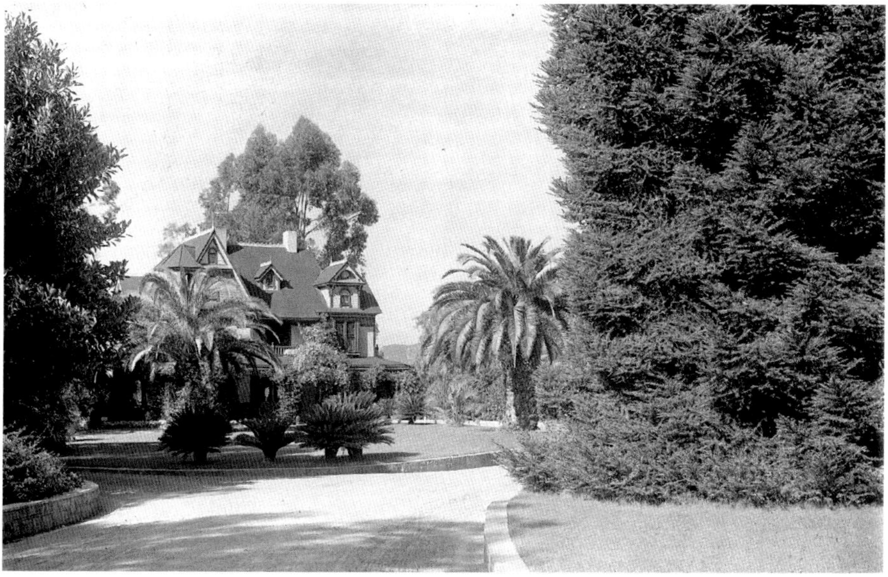

The A.K. Smiley home in Cañon Crest Park. Together, Alfred K. Smiley and his twin, Albert H. Smiley, owned more than two hundred acres of Redlands hillside above Cypress. The lushly landscaped park was open to the public and drew tourists by the thousands to take in the flora and fauna, as well as the spectacular view of the San Bernardino Mountains. Smiley niece Ruth Smiley Drake and her husband, A. B. Drake, later lived here until it was destroyed by fire in 1954.

Once their homesteads were taken care of, the Smileys turned to town. They saw the need for a library and got a committee started. Within a few years, they had secured land for a downtown park and a private loan for the library building. The Smiley twins and their brother, Daniel, were successful men but not wealthy. Their willingness to place themselves in debt for the good of the city became an example for all to follow.

Multimillionaire Albert C. Burrage ordered his Boston architect to design his seventeen-thousand-square-foot, thirty-six-room Redlands cottage with a veranda on all sides. Located above Crescent Avenue, the grounds were also open to the public for a time. The Burrages visited their Redlands home for only a few winters, yet they left their mark as well. His wife, Alice Hathaway Haskell Burrage, gave the money for the building of the current Trinity Episcopal Church in memory of her mother. Mr. Burrage helped organize the University Club and gave it land for a clubhouse. In 1906, he rushed $100,000 to San Francisco to aid the earthquake and fire victims.

The current owner of the property, Tim Rochford, continues the Burrage legacy today. Rochford has partnered with Micah House, an after-school program for children and youth through twelfth grade. The Micah House website notes that the "Burrage Mansion and its 17-acre grounds will provide a sanctuary, a place for our children to get away without cost-prohibitive and time-prohibitive travel. The mansion is a connection to a simpler era, and the Micah House kids will have the opportunity to play, reflect, learn, laugh and grow in this safe, beautiful and serene environment."

In 1899, John and Helen Cheney Kimberly began to spend winters in Redlands. John and his brothers had turned their Neenah, Wisconsin paper mill into the internationally known paper company Kimberly-Clark. In 1905, the Kimberlys bought a French chateau on the hill and named it Kimberly Crest. Helen Kimberly launched herself into Redlands civic affairs with the energy to match her husband's business ventures, and the town was the beneficiary.

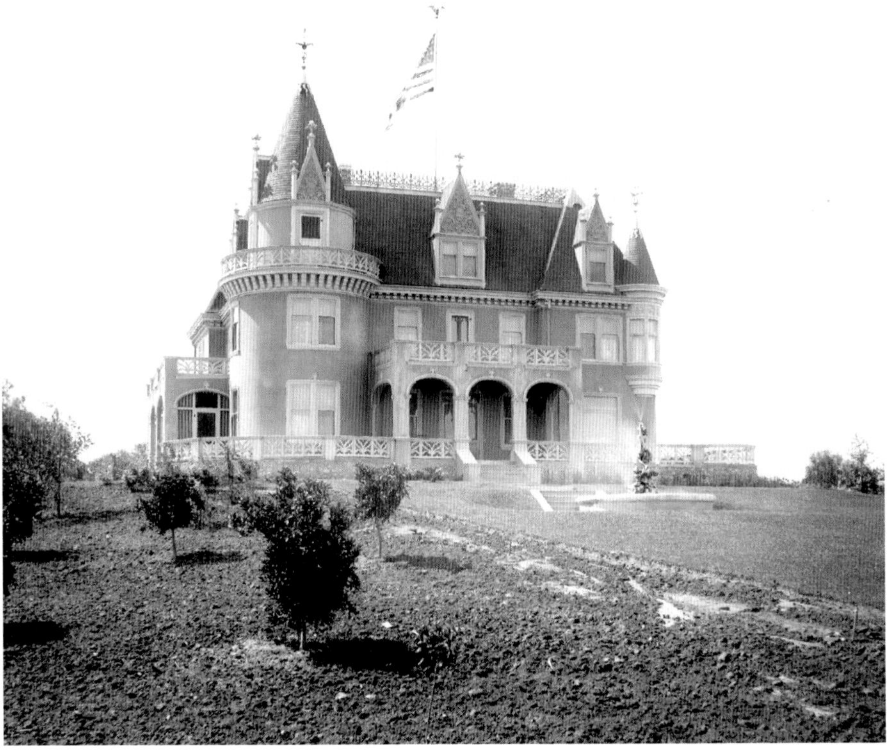

Cornelia A. Hill, a widow from New York, built this beautiful French chateau in 1897. In 1905, Helen and John Kimberly bought the home and its acreage on the hill next to Prospect Park and named it Kimberly Crest. Mrs. Kimberly went on to enhance the landscape with Mediterranean-style plantings, pergolas and terraces. Kimberly daughter, Mary Emma Shirk, donated the house and gardens to the people of Redlands by bequeathing Kimberly Crest to a nonprofit Redlands corporation upon her death in 1979.

The Kimberlys joined the First Congregational Church, setting an example for others by generously supporting it financially. Mrs. Kimberly opened her checkbook during the early, lean years of the Community Music Association, rescuing it from disaster. Mrs. Kimberly and her daughter, Mary Kimberly Shirk, saw to it that the Contemporary Club debt for its original clubhouse was paid off, and they carried out many improvements and modernizations to that facility.

Helen Kimberly saw a need to train girls to take their place in the world, so she organized the Kimberly Juniors, an organization still civilizing young women to this day. Mrs. Kimberly's name became synonymous with all that was genteel in turn-of-the-twentieth-century America. Her daughter, Mrs. Shirk, carried on the tradition and left the family's beautiful house and grounds (supported by an endowment) to the people of Redlands upon her own death. Mary Shirk wanted to be sure that future generations would understand and experience life as it was in her mother's day, so Kimberly Crest was left with furnishings and household items intact.

Thomas Y. and E. Clarissa Combs England became winter residents of Redlands in 1887. England had made his fortune in the leather business in Philadelphia. They purchased sixty acres above Highland Avenue and began to develop a botanical garden similar in style to the Smiley's Cañon Crest Park. Mrs. England is said to have guided much of the design and labor, as Mr. England was busy with his business interests. The sculpted roadways and terraced stone walls of Prospect Park became an important stop for the tallyho and surrey passengers who came to tour Cañon Crest Park. Maintained by the private funding of the England family, it was generously open to the public until the time of the Depression.

The Diamond-Studded Atmosphere of Early Redlands

In a town such as Redlands, reminders of the past are all around us. The beautiful parks, skyline trees and fine samples of Victorian architecture require little imagination to reconstruct the way things used to be. While many of the homes from our golden age—the millionaire and mansion era of the turn of the twentieth century—are still showplaces today, others have been lost to fire or disrepair.

One of the most spectacular homes of this period was the Henry Fisher estate on Highland Avenue. Photographs of the home and its occupants fill an entire chapter of Bill Moore's book, *Redlands Yesterdays*.

Henry brought his wife and son, John (also known as Fritz), to visit Redlands in 1890. They stayed at the Terracina Hotel and later came back to live in a cottage they built on the grounds. Having sold his Standard Oil interests in 1892, Fisher was a wealthy man. Unfortunately, Fisher's wife, Mary Clark Fisher, died in 1893. The probable cause of her death was tuberculosis, since we know that many invalids with that disease came to the Terracina Hotel in hopes of recovering their health. What happened next was to affect the Redlands social and philanthropic scene for decades to come.

Henry Fisher the widower was fifty years old. His imposing stature and full beard make him a recognizable figure in old photographs. Henry married Marion Josephine Thomas the next year. Marion was born in 1871 and was twenty-three years old when she married Henry Fisher. Not only that, she was also the younger sister of Henry's son's wife. Needless to say, the occasion elevated a few eyebrows. Together, Henry and Marion produced four children, three girls (one died in infancy) and a boy. They built their magnificent home on the northeast corner of Highland Avenue and San Mateo Street in 1897–98 and furnished it with antiques, Persian rugs and artwork from all over the world. The

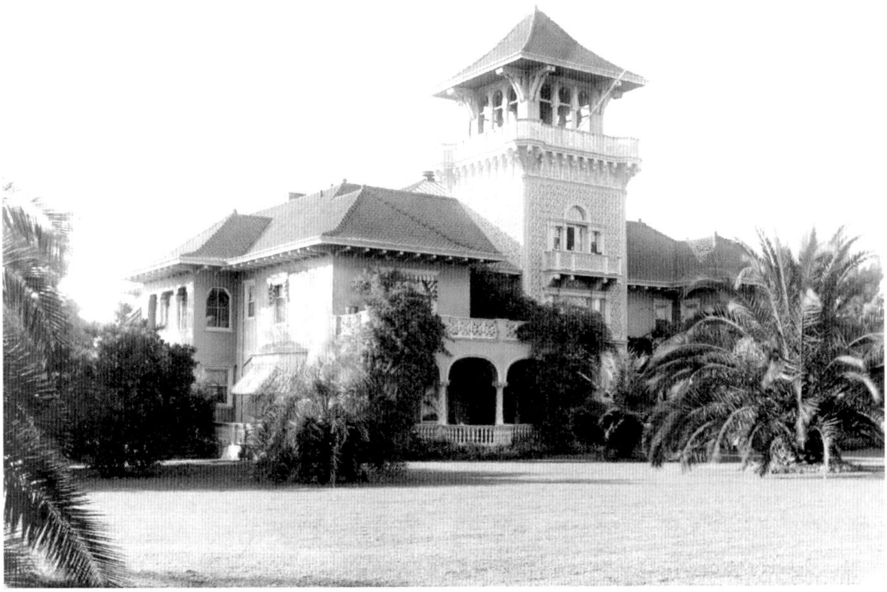

Henry Fisher, a Pennsylvania oil pioneer, made a second fortune in electricity and transportation in Redlands. Fisher built this marvelous mansion on the northeast corner of Highland Avenue and San Mateo Street in 1897–98. The gardens were elaborately landscaped in keeping with the design of the house.

Fisher home was the center of Redlands' social whirl, and Marion was a society leader.

Henry continued to make money. He backed H.H. Sinclair's development of the first electrical systems. Their power and light companies joined others to become the Southern California Edison Company. Fisher also developed the electric streetcar system in Redlands and took it across the Santa Ana River wash to San Bernardino. He sold to Henry E. Huntington in 1908 for a tidy profit.

The Henry Fisher house was Moorish in style, built around a central atrium that was several stories tall and capped with a stained-glass roof. Alhambra-type arches, heavily decorated, surrounded the tiled atrium and provided the backdrop for the Fisher's extraordinary parties.

The *Golden Jubilee Book* of 1938 had this to say about happenings in the year 1905: "Elegant households on the heights…The dazzling Henry Fisher residence on West Highland, where lavish parties were served by Los Angeles caterers in a diamond-studded atmosphere, amazed the bourgeois community."

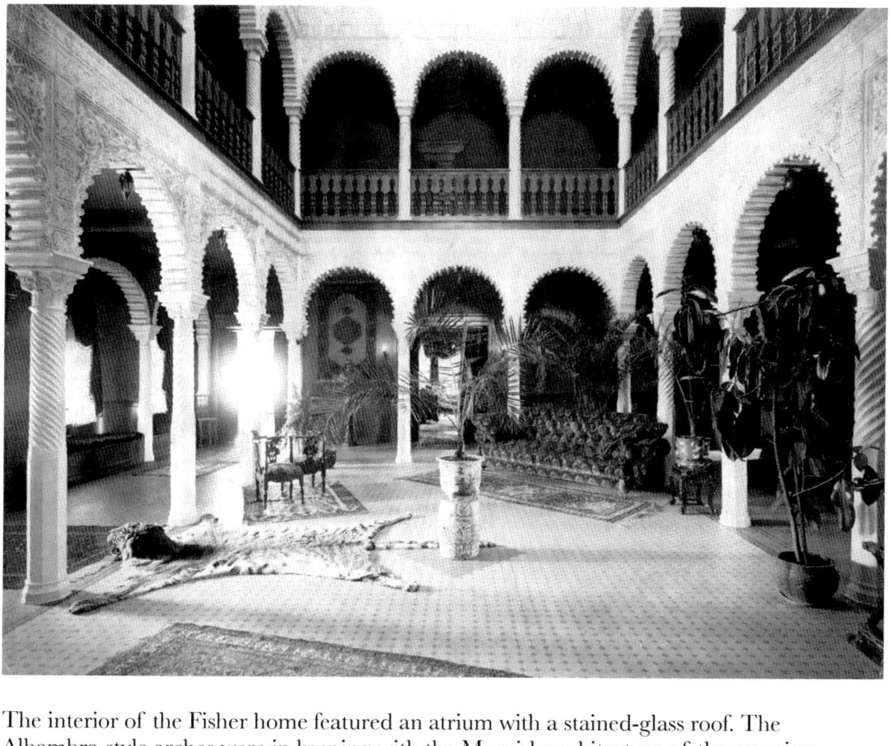

The interior of the Fisher home featured an atrium with a stained-glass roof. The Alhambra-style arches were in keeping with the Moorish architecture of the mansion. Marion Fisher often used the space for elaborate parties.

L.E. Nelson, in *Only One Redlands*, wrote, "Her [Marion Fisher] social adeptness became proverbial. At her Flower Cotillion on New Year's Eve [1907] the guests were modest violets, queenly lilies, dashing American Beauties, saucy brown-eyed Susans, blushing cherry blossoms, pure white hyacinths, fragrant carnations and dainty lilies of the valley." Marion Fisher was a talented actress and singer. She performed in many of the local productions at the Wyatt Opera House and was responsible for bringing big name talent to perform there as well.

In 1907, Harold Bell Wright spent a short time as pastor of the Christian Church in Redlands. A few years later, he caused the local tongues to wag as he published his novel, *The Eyes of the World*, with its thinly veiled references to society life in Redlands. Many believed that Marion had inspired Bell's more denigrating descriptions of life lived to excess in his fictional Fairlands.

While there was truth to the descriptions of extravagant entertainment, it was also true that Marion Fisher devoted much of her time and resources to the philanthropic needs of the community. Her ability to attract musicians and actors to perform at the Wyatt set the tone for the future success of the Redlands Bowl organizers.

Fashionable addresses come and go much the same as fashionable dress styles. After World War I, the wealthy families began to leave, lured to other places. The Fishers maintained a business interest in Redlands, but Henry and Marion moved on to Santa Barbara in the early 1920s. The house eventually fell into disrepair and was torn down, the property subdivided. The Fisher's high, stone garden wall still lines the east side of San Mateo Street in the block running up to Highland Avenue.

They must have always regarded Redlands as home. Henry died in 1929 and Marion in 1954. Both are buried at Hillside Memorial Park in Redlands.

REDLANDS CAN REMEMBER BEAUTIFUL PARKS OF THE PAST

In 1895, Redlands was less than ten years old, yet it already boasted sidewalks, streetcars and beautifully curbed streets. There were also three unusual parks, none of which exists today.

On May 10, 1895, the *Redlands Daily Facts* boasted, "Redlands is destined to be the center of the greatest system of parks on the coast, each having its own identity." The three parks were Cañon Crest Park, Tremont Park and Fredalba Park; all three were compliments of the Smiley brothers.

Alfred Smiley, a well-to-do New Yorker, brought his family to Los Angeles for a vacation in 1888 and was persuaded to visit a new community called Redlands. He was so taken with the place that he arranged at once to buy fifty acres on the southwest side of town. He then cabled his identical twin brother Albert. Albert was about to leave for a winter in Palestine, but his brother's cable changed his plans. Alfred wired that he had found the "promised land" in California.

Together the brothers purchased another two hundred acres. On their ridge of land west of Highland Avenue and Serpentine, they built two large homes and surrounded them with gardens pretty much unparalleled anywhere. The Smiley's called their creation Cañon Crest Park, and it was destined to become famous.

Less well known was the Smiley acreage on the south side of San Timoteo Canyon known as Tremont Park. Tremont Park was thought to have real potential for a resort development. The brothers planted a eucalyptus grove and laid out four miles of road. From the top, the three-thousand-foot elevation offered dramatic valley and mountain views. The lack of adequate water led to the abandonment of their plans.

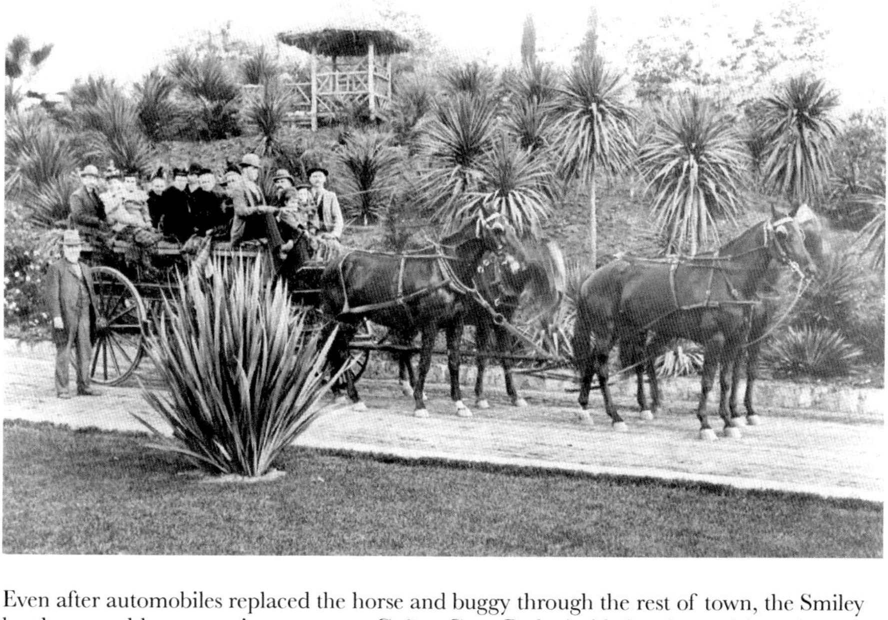

Even after automobiles replaced the horse and buggy through the rest of town, the Smiley brothers would not permit cars to tour Cañon Crest Park. A ride in a large sightseeing coach, called a tallyho, was a popular alternative.

A trip into the San Bernardino Mountains via the City Creek Toll Road (now known as Route 330) introduced the brothers to an area reminiscent of their beloved Adirondacks. In 1895, they bought 262 acres and built Fredalba Park (a creative combination of "Alfred" and "Albert"). A restaurant and several cottages were built. The Smileys' plans for a hotel and electric railway to scale the mountain never materialized. Fredalba enjoyed a brief boom as a resort and later as a town for families of sawmill workers. The demise of the lumber industry and a change in the road left Fredalba to languish as a quiet community of summer homes.

You can find Fredalba, and the residential area called Smiley Park, by driving north on Highway 330. Turn right on Fredalba Road just before Running Springs. The Smileys sold their property in the 1920s, but their layout of scenic, wooded drives exists the same today. In the 1950s, Dale and (Alma) Gene Bauer bought a plot in this mountainside area for a summer cabin. Gene, an artist, spent the next half-century planting waves of daffodils throughout their five-acre parcel. Following the spirit of the Smileys, the Bauers opened their property to the public for three weeks every spring. Countless visitors have been enthralled by the living paintings planted bulb

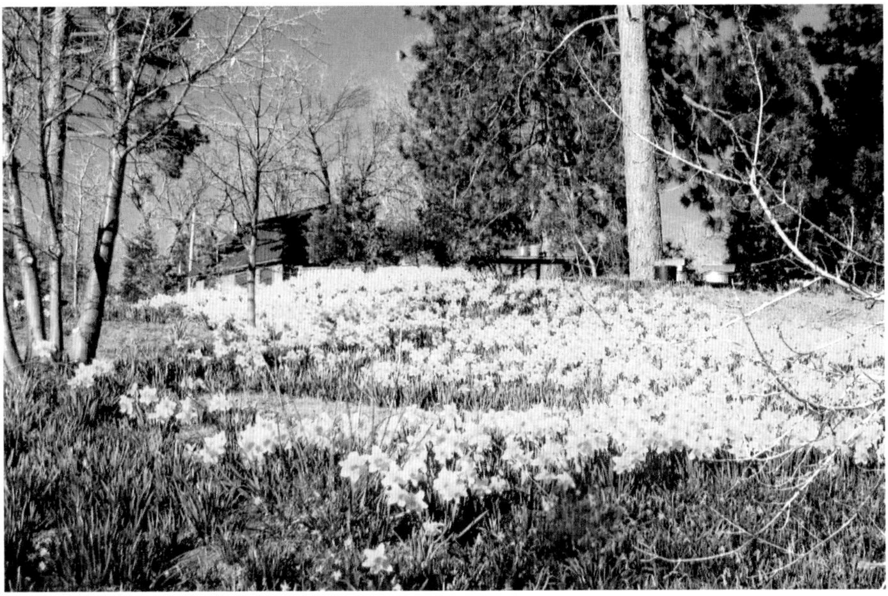

For more than fifty years, artist Gene Bauer planted her five-acre property in the mountainside community of Smiley Park with swaths of daffodil bulbs. For decades, until the early 2000s, she invited the public to enjoy her creations for three weeks every season. *Courtesy Rhea-Frances Tetley.*

by bulb by Gene Bauer. Wildfires and time have taken their toll, and the Bauer garden is no longer open for viewing.

Meanwhile, Cañon Crest Park was making a name for itself. Alfred and Albert Smiley spent nearly $500,000 to construct their park. More than five miles of scenic roadways were landscaped with more than 1,200 varieties of trees and plants. Dozens of small gazebos, called "spooners," based on those at the Smiley Mohonk Mountain House Resort in New York, were scattered around the property at strategic viewpoints. The plant material matured quickly in our mild climate, and the combination of lush vegetation and spectacular views became world-renowned.

Cañon Crest Park became so famous that it attracted between fifteen thousand and twenty-five thousand visitors per year. Presidents William McKinley and Theodore Roosevelt came to see the views. Ordinary folk joined the famous, such as the Carnegies, Rockefellers, Harrimans and Vanderbilts.

The Smileys allowed no automobiles to go through their park. Photographs in William G. Moore's book *Redlands Yesterdays* show tallyho carriages lined up

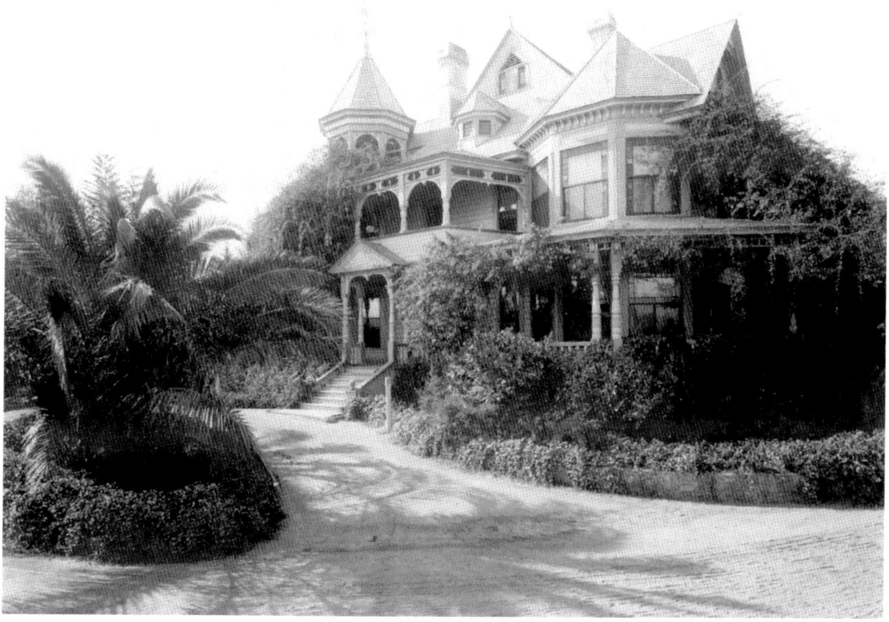

Alfred Smiley built his home in Cañon Crest a little to the east of his brother's and slightly down the hill. The entire property was planted with orange groves, trees and ornamental plants. Cut-stone curbs and walls supported roads with wonderful views. Small gazebos called "spooners" offered visitors the chance to stop and admire the scenery.

at the Southern Pacific depot in Redlands. These open-sided, horse-drawn trams carried nine to fifteen passengers. It was not unusual for one hundred people a day to take the two-hour tour.

Later known as Smiley Heights, Cañon Crest Park was maintained and operated at the personal expense of the Smiley family. It was open to the public free of charge. In return for their generosity, the city gave the Smiley family a special cut rate on their property taxes. In 1936, the Depression prompted a shortsighted city council to withdraw the tax break even though Smiley descendant Ruth Smiley Sanborn Drake and her family told the city that they could not afford to operate the park without the tax arrangement. The city refused to budge, and the family was forced to close the park.

Over the years, numerous unsuccessful efforts were made to convert the area to a city park. The two Smiley mansions were gone, Albert's destroyed by fire and Alfred's by the wrecking ball. Finally, in 1962, the Smiley family offered to sell the entire property to the city for $200,000. The city manager asked, "What would we do with it?" and refused the offer.

The Smiley family was shocked and saddened. Their generosity should have ensured the preservation of this remarkable reminder of a kinder, gentler era. Instead, the land was subdivided, and all but one thirteen-acre ridge top parcel became small home sites.

A few years later, Prospect Park faced the same fate, but this time, the town rallied to preserve the past.

Colonel Greene's Dream Mansion Was a Tribute Befitting the Copper Baron

Once upon a time, there was a man who rose from obscurity, playing real-life cowboys and Indians along the way, to become one of the richest men in America. His copper-rich hole in the ground in northern Mexico led to an only slightly smaller hole in the ground in Redlands. This is the story of Colonel Greene's Mansion.

Colonel William Greene was one of the most colorful characters of Redlands' millionaire-and-mansion era. He graced the local folklore for fifty years beyond his time, yet he never lived here. Greene was worth more than $80 million in 1906. At the age of fifty-two, he was ready to build a home befitting his status as a major copper baron. His mining town, Cananea, Mexico, forty miles south of the Arizona border, had grown from zero to a population of twenty-five thousand people. Greene's home there, called the Big House, was large but not ostentatious.

Greene heard about Redlands in 1906 from a relative of A.K. Smiley. During a train trip, Greene was persuaded to detour through Redlands. Frank and Bill Moore devoted several *Redlands Daily Facts* "With a Grain of Salt" columns to Greene. In 1950, they reported:

> *On arriving here they* [Greene and friends] *took a carriage and drove to Cañon Crest Park* [Smiley Heights], *through the Cypress avenue entrance, and along the drives which yield the grandest sweep of majestic and yet charming scenery. Mr. Greene could not restrain his admiration and as they wound along the Serpentine Drive he exclaimed: "This is the finest thing I ever saw. The world does not hold its equal…"*
>
> *Before many months had passed the man from Cananea owned all of the land above Crescent avenue between the property of the Smileys to the west and the property of Albert Burrage the Boston copper king to the east.*

Greene wasted no time. Within two months of the visit to Redlands, Los Angeles architect John C. Austin was hired to design, and C.J. Kubach and Company was engaged to build Greene's Redlands residence. (Both of these men would be involved in the design and building of several famous Los Angeles structures.) And what a residence it was to be. The *Facts* reported that "[t]he massive pile will be three and four stories high with one tower at the front 70 feet high. The general dimensions of the structure will be 134 by 126 feet. It is to be provided with extensive plumbing and wired for electricity."

The house was to overlook San Timoteo Canyon on one side and the San Bernardino Valley on the other—a 360-degree view. The Smileys offered their assistance to develop the landscape so that Greene's property could be viewed by the public as an extension of Cañon Crest Park. In the early spring of 1907, Greene was so anxious to begin construction that builder Kubach was ordered to begin the foundation before the plans were even finished. Architect Austin was set up to supervise the operation and was given joint control of a $50,000 bank account. Train cars loaded with lumber, steel rods, steel netting and cement began rolling into Redlands at the rate of several carloads per day.

Thirty wagon teams hauled the material from the rail yards and sand and gravel from a special quarry in the wash. Two hundred men were employed in the excavation and construction. About $250,000 was expected to be spent to

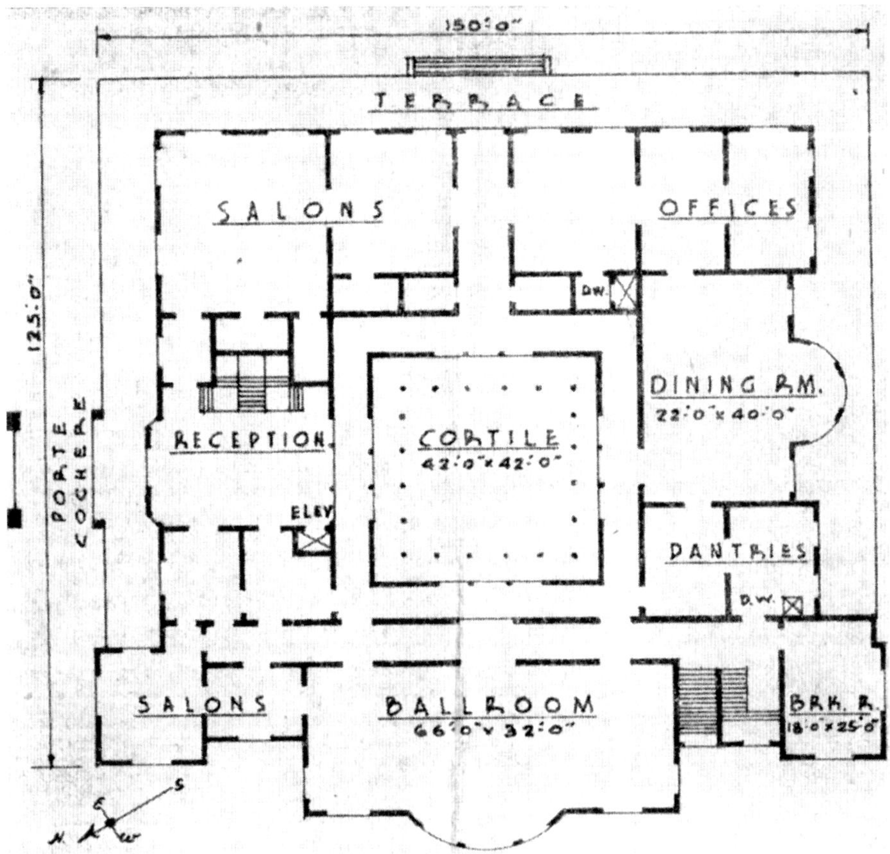

In 1906, copper baron William Greene hired Los Angeles architect John C. Austin to design an imposing mansion for Greene's property high on a Redlands ridge. The home was never built beyond the foundation. In 1953, *Redlands Daily Facts* editor Frank Moore interviewed Austin and asked Redlands architect Ben Rabe to re-create the floor plan. This would have been just the first of three stories above ground, built on a massive basement housing the kitchen and utilities.

erect the building. The lavish finishing work would cost hundreds of thousands more. By August 1907, the foundations for Greene's Mansion had been laid, and the forms were ready for pouring the walls of the first story.

In 1953, Frank and Bill Moore interviewed architect Austin, who said:

> *During 1907 Mr. Greene plunged heavily in Wall Street and when the slump came in the fall he pledged his Cananea stock to the Knickerbocker bank on one-day notes. The bank found it necessary to foreclose on him and he lost control of the Cananea mines.*

> *...Greene came to my office in Los Angeles. While he looked at the plans for his house he did not seem interested in them. He said that he was giving a party that night at the Alexandria Hotel for the Mexican ambassador and asked if I would like to come. It would be a full dress affair, of course, he added.*
>
> *I went and it was a royal banquet indeed. There were roses on the walls, and under the top of the glass dining table there were ferns, and live, swimming fish. With each course of dinner there was a different wine. The chef personally brought into the room each main dish and carried it around the table, showing it off, before serving.*
>
> *Little did I know that I was paying for that banquet. Mr. Greene asked me how much money was in our joint bank account and I told him I thought the amount was about $5,000. The next day I...found that there was only $100 left in our account. Apparently the party had been paid for with the construction funds.*

For fifty years, Greene's Mansion engendered the stories of local folklore. Boys explored with candles, scared the socks off one another and chased bats with tennis rackets. Lovers took moonlit strolls and pushed the envelope of propriety. University of Redlands fraternities held their initiation ceremonies in its depths. Students brought beer kegs and noisy voices and built bonfires. The corpses of fallen dogs warned mothers to keep their young children from playing on top of the platform. The building's only sanctioned use was for Easter Sunrise services.

Several attempts failed to build a hotel on top of the foundation, and in 1953, with developers eyeing the property, Greene's Mansion was declared an attractive nuisance. The owner, E.J. Raehn, agreed to demolish the structure. A five-thousand-pound steel wrecking ball pounded away for a whole week. The above-ground concrete was removed (and the pieces thrown over the other side of Sunset Drive into San Timoteo Canyon), but much of the underground walls and footings (some five feet thick and steel reinforced) had to be left, the spaces filled in with dirt.

Of the forty or so homes that occupy the property today, several have been affected by the subterranean remains. One house had to be "pontooned" across a part of it. Swimming pools cannot be dug because the concrete is a mere eighteen inches down. Fortunately, Californians don't expect their homes to have basements these days.

The copper baron's legacy lives on.

Redlands' Walls Were Not Always What They Seemed

Good fences make good neighbors.

–Robert Frost

When is a wall not a wall? Homebuilder Walter Nordhoff took up that question in 1900 in a colorful dispute with the Redlands City Hall. Nordhoff's new home was conveniently located on the route of the Smiley Heights electric car. From the corner in front of his house, Nordhoff could step into the streetcar, take the short ride downtown to the train depot on Orange Street and, in about an hour, arrive in Los Angeles to take care of his many business affairs. The price to be paid for this convenience was the noise of a streetcar that ran all day and into the night. It was too much for wife Sarah Nordhoff and her new baby, so Walter surrounded his Pacific Street home with a high rock wall.

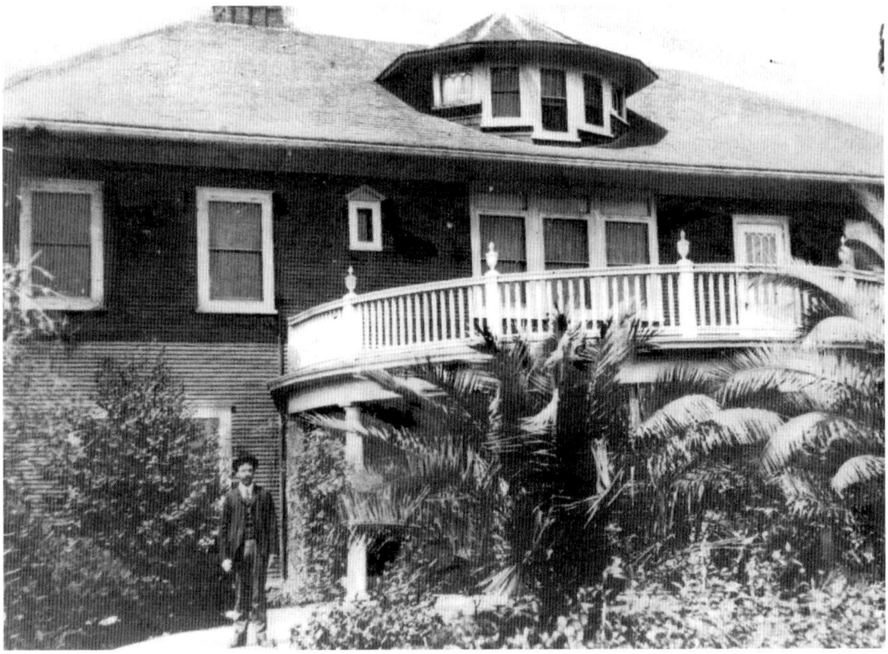

Walter Nordhoff stands in front of his home on Pacific Street. From a nearby corner, he could step on the streetcar for a short ride to the Santa Fe station downtown. There he could board a train and be in Los Angeles to conduct his business affairs in about an hour.

However, there was an ordinance against the building of such walls, and the City of Redlands directed Nordhoff to tear it down. Nordhoff refused, and the wall became a metaphor of his enigmatic life.

Walter Nordhoff, sandwiched between famous father and even more famous son, both named Charles, was a man of privacy. His father, Charles Nordhoff, was an early proponent of life in California, having written *California for Health, Pleasure and Residence* in 1873. Walter's son, Charles Bernard Nordhoff, is most remembered for coauthoring the *Mutiny on the Bounty* trilogy with James Norman Hall in the 1930s. Frederick Bromberger's Fortnightly Paper, "The Nordhoff Trilogy," chronicles the lives of these three men and their connection to Redlands.

Young Walter achieved a measure of success as a correspondent for his father's newspaper, the *New York Herald*. He was posted in Paris and London, and his wife, Sarah Whitall, gave birth to their first child, Charles Bernard, in London in 1887. Three years later, the young family found themselves at what must have seemed the opposite end of the earth, Baja California.

Charles Nordhoff Sr. had purchased a large tract of land just south of Ensenada in about 1888, and he persuaded his son, Walter, to join him in the development and management of the property, Rancho del Cabo de Todos Santos. This joint endeavor fell apart when Walter began building a large house, Ramajal, away from the coast and dependable water supply. Charles left for Santa Barbara and never returned.

Sarah traveled between the primitive life in Todos Santos and rented homes in Los Angeles, Coronado and Pasadena. Two more children were born, and her health was always a problem. In 1897, she visited a new town amid the orange groves. The schools were good, the climate was dry and healthy and connections to the rest of the world were an easy train ride away. Thus the Nordhoffs came to Redlands.

Walter purchased a large piece of property on the corner of Pacific and Cedar Streets and built a permanent home for his family. Bromberger noted, "He was selling cattle at $24 a head and must have had some good years before 1898 to be able to gather the $15,000 for the new house and barn."

Walter continued to build his exotic home in Todos Santos, and the family joined him there from time to time. Sons Charlie and Franklin brought some of their Redlands friends along for hunting and fishing adventures. The ranch passed out of Nordhoff hands after World War I.

Walter began a new career about 1912. He started a tile making business near National City, California. His company, the California China Products Company, created tile used to line the dome of the California Building in

San Diego's Balboa Park, the floor of the Santa Fe Railroad Station and the ceiling of the Globe Theater, all built for the 1915 Pan-American Exposition. The tile company went out of business in 1917 but established a precedent for the use of Spanish-influenced tile as part of a new Southern California Hispanic style in architecture.

The family sold their Redlands home in 1916 and wandered the world before settling in Santa Barbara in 1921. In his eighth decade of life, having satisfied the yen for adventure and wanderlust, Walter returned to his creative side and once again picked up the pen. His first book, *The Journey of the Flame*, was accepted for publication in 1932. This was followed by a second, *Rico, Bandit and Dictator*, in 1934 when he was seventy-nine.

Both novels were published under the name Antonio del Fierro Blanco, as Walter wished to have no part of the sensationalist publicity that had followed the lives of his father and son. In fact, even the editor and publisher of his books had no clue that Fierro Blanco was a pseudonym. Novelist Scott O'Dell, in his preface to the second edition of *The Journey of the Flame*, wrote of the mystery that surrounded the author and the tight secrecy that was finally broken by Walter:

> *He was just what he appeared to be and wished to remain—a man entirely too busy in his youth to follow his natural heritage of writing. A gentleman of eighty, content now to live quietly among his flowers after long and adventurous years, sharing the spirit of Juan Colorado known as The Flame, who like an earlier hidalgo was born with a strong right arm, a gift of laughter and a sense that the world was mad.*

Bromberger concluded:

> *Then a strange journey occurred. Walter, dead at eighty two in 1937, came back to Hillside Memorial Park. Charlie, aged sixty, followed in 1947. Wife and mother, Sarah, sickly all her life, arrived here in 1951, aged eighty-nine. Brother Franklin pursued them in 1956, Charlie's sister Mary in 1977 and his daughter Jane in 1992. None of them had lived in Redlands for many years, yet each must have decided that this should be his resting place…Why…? Maybe this is the answer: Redlands is home.*

And the wall? It is still there. The city decided on a compromise: the wall was declared to be not a wall but rather a terrace for climbing roses. Who says you cannot fight city hall?

Watchorn Led the Way of Volunteerism in Redlands

Whether you think it takes a village or a thousand points of light, the spirit of the volunteer is one of the things that makes this country great.

Robert and Alma Watchorn were such spirits. Some people give of their time and some give of their money, but the Watchorns gave of both. Robert Watchorn is a reminder that one can become a great American without being born here. Robert Watchorn was born in Alfreton, England, in 1858. Son of a coal miner, he was himself sent to work in the mines at the age of eleven. The hours were long, and the work was grueling and dangerous, but he found enough energy to attend night classes to extend his meager schooling. Watchorn immigrated to the United States in 1880. He found work as a coal miner in Pennsylvania and became a naturalized citizen. His involvement with the United Mine Workers of America led to his becoming its first secretary.

Over the next few decades, Watchorn held a variety of political appointments, including that of the United States commissioner of immigration at Ellis Island from 1905 to 1909. He took the job of treasurer of Union Oil Company in 1909 and by 1916 was president of his own Watchorn Oil and Gas Company.

The Watchorns moved to Redlands, built a large home and began to look for ways to volunteer. Watchorn had made a fortune in the Oklahoma oil fields, but tragedy marred the success. Their only son, Emory, was an aviator

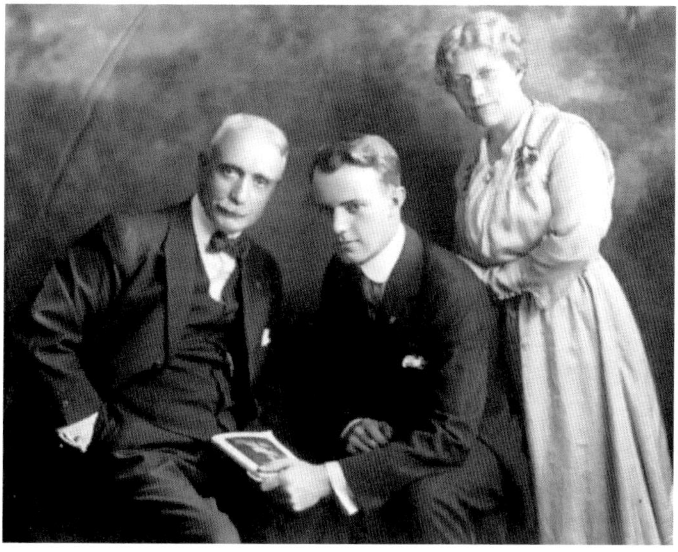

Alma and Robert Watchorn pose with their son, Emory, in about 1915.

in World War I. The younger Watchorn survived several heroic battles but lost the war to ill health in 1921 at the age of twenty-five. As grieving parents often do, the Watchorns sought a fitting memorial to their son, and Redlands benefited in three ways.

In 1925, the Watchorns donated a set of Westminster chimes to be played from the tower of the Methodist church on the corner of Olive and Cajon. The Watchorn Chimes faithfully tolled on the quarter hour and accompanied the Redlands High School Graduation exercises at the Redlands Bowl for more than forty years, until the church burned down in June 1967.

Phyllis Irshay, in her book *The Pride and Glory of the Town*, told us more of the Watchorn generosity: "Robert and Alma J. Watchorn entered into a memorandum of agreement with the City Council tendering the gift of the Lincoln Memorial or Shrine to the city in May, 1931...The total paid by Robert Watchorn was $42,000—and this at the height of the depression!"

A committee of community volunteers worked with Watchorn and the architect Elmer Grey as they designed the octagonal building with entrance flanked by granite walls inscribed with excerpts from Lincoln's speeches. Granite patio wings with fountain and benches were added in 1937. In 1998, the museum was expanded, and these patio elements were preserved as part of the new construction.

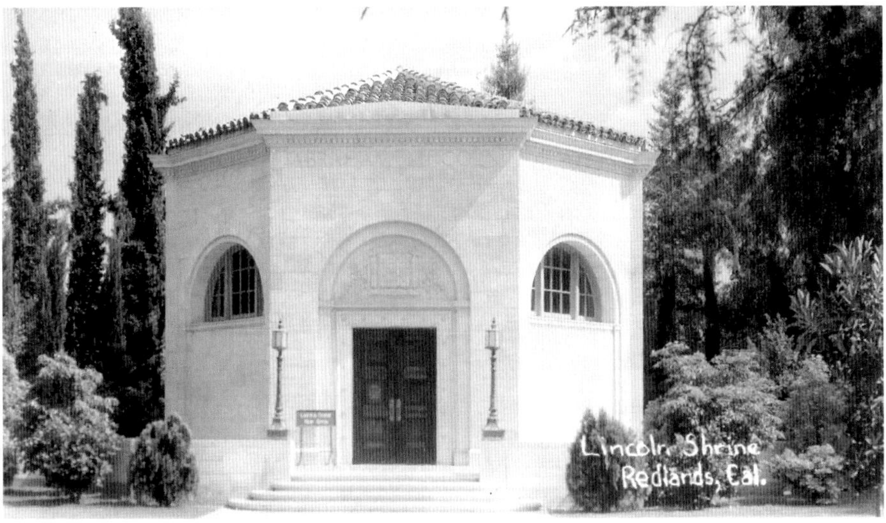

Alma and Robert Watchorn donated the money for the Lincoln Shrine, built in 1932. The original octagonal building, located in Smiley Park behind the library, was enlarged in 1998. Dedicated to the memory of their son, Emory, it houses the only collection west of the Mississippi devoted to Abraham Lincoln and the Civil War.

Emory Watchorn had inspired his father's donation of Lincoln memorabilia. In his autobiography, Watchorn wrote:

> *On one occasion, after a few months' visit to England in prewar times, he* [Emory] *said to me, "Dad! I think the reason the English people have such a limited respect for America and Americans is due to the fact that they are kept in ignorance of the actual America. I think…if they could be made acquainted with the big, outstanding fact that the kind-hearted, pure-minded Lincoln is America's greatest hero, all England would come to love Lincoln too, and…they could not fail to appreciate America also.*
>
> *…"What more appropriate character could be found among the very great men of the world to be chosen for the purpose of promoting 'charity for all men and all nations, and malice towards none.'*
>
> *…"All men everywhere should know Abraham Lincoln. He was acquainted with grief, and the whole world would be the richer by knowing how uncomplainingly he bore it, and how nobly he lived, and how his passing grieved the nation he had kept from deplorable disruption.*
>
> *"Being well acquainted is the vestibule to good will, and good will precludes rancorous strife. It is inconceivable that any nation could dread America if Abraham Lincoln's life and purpose were fully revealed to it…*
>
> *"It will be a very happy event for me if I can be the means of introducing him to a few, especially to those of my native town, whose hearts I know beat in true unison with the ideals of Lincoln…With the extension of these ideals there will undoubtedly be a better world, based as they are on the principle of the golden rule."*

Watchorn also described the philosophy behind his generosity: "After having provided for his own immediate necessities, a man's first duty is to consider the welfare of others before he goes about the business of pulling down his meager barns to build greater ones."

In making their third large gift to the city of Redlands, Mrs. Watchorn said quietly, "We consider this not a charity but an investment," as she handed a check for $200,000 to the University of Redlands to build the Watchorn Hall of Music.

The legacy of Robert and Alma Watchorn should inspire us all to remember the ideals of Lincoln. It is a uniquely American event that the lives of Lincoln, the boy from Illinois, and Watchorn, the boy from the English coal mines, have intertwined in a way that helps us all appreciate what it is to be an American.

Part V
Ordinary People Made Extraordinary Contributions to Redlands History

Turn-of-the-twentieth-century Redlands was a town divided by social class. Upper mixed with middle class when performing church and civic duties, but the two social circles were generally separate. A large middle class resided in the Victorian homes and cottages dotting the streets closest to downtown. Then, as now, the more expensive homes were to be found in the hills. Highland Avenue attracted the largest number of these homes in the early years, leading some to label it "the butler belt."

Though the upper- and middle-class social circles were separate, social behaviors and traditions were similar. Edith Parker Hinckley, Redlands historian and contemporary of those times, wrote:

> *A certain formality and elegance of behavior existed in the days of Redlands' adolescence that corresponded to the ornateness of the architecture. The ladies all had regular "at home" days when they expected their friends to call, duly hatted and gloved. It is true that a carriage, with a coachman in livery and perhaps a footman behind, drawn by a spanking team of bays, had a poignant distinction that no mere machine can equal…*
>
> *…A boy called his lady friend "Miss" until they were engaged or about to be. The girls wore white shirtwaists and long skirts that had to be held up on the dusty streets. They also wore corset covers and long black stockings, but of course these were never mentioned! The boys wore their hair longer and they were hampered by high stiff choker collars with four-in-hand ties. On the whole, the young people were not as attractive as they are now,*

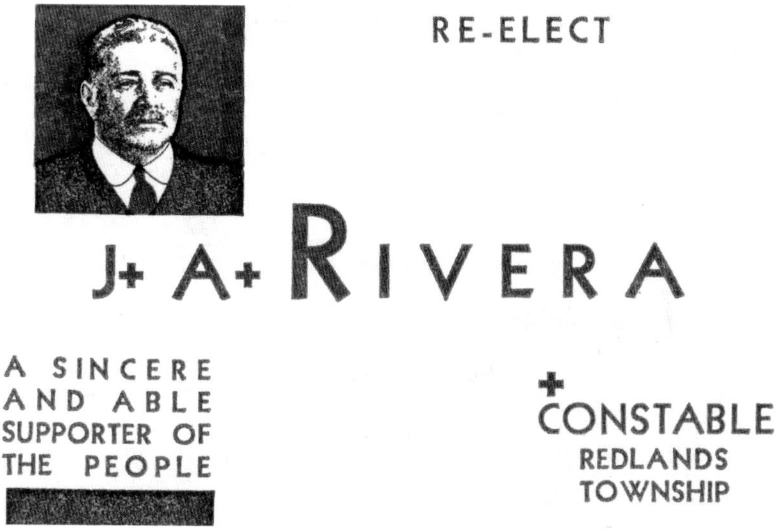

Jose Rivera served as constable for the city of Redlands for nearly fifty years. Easily reelected every time he ran for office, Rivera was respected by all members of the community.

> *especially the girls, because they were without benefit of beauty shops, and faces and hair were as God made them.*

By 1900, the population of the town was 5,500, and the ones who were not millionaires tended to stick around longer. One of the more interesting residents of this category was the first constable, Jose Rivera. When Redlands was ready to incorporate in 1888, Rivera got into an argument with one of the candidates for constable. Rivera had not planned to run for office but jokingly bet that he would win in a contest between the two. Scipio Craig, of the *Citrograph*, got wind of this and promoted Rivera to the point that he got more votes than the other six candidates combined.

Rivera turned out to be the right man, in the right place, for the job. He was resoundingly reelected. His devotion to the city and his job prevailed against offers for higher positions elsewhere. When Rivera retired in 1935, having served the city for *forty-seven* years, his parting comments indicate his wisdom and strength of character: "My policy…has never been to expect trouble. I never did believe in hunting for criminals with a sawed off shotgun. I prefer to go alone when trouble is reported and invariably I find that the bad man is more sensible than the people who have reported him."

For nearly fifty years, Constable Rivera brought justice and fairness to the community. He was known to carry outstanding warrants around in

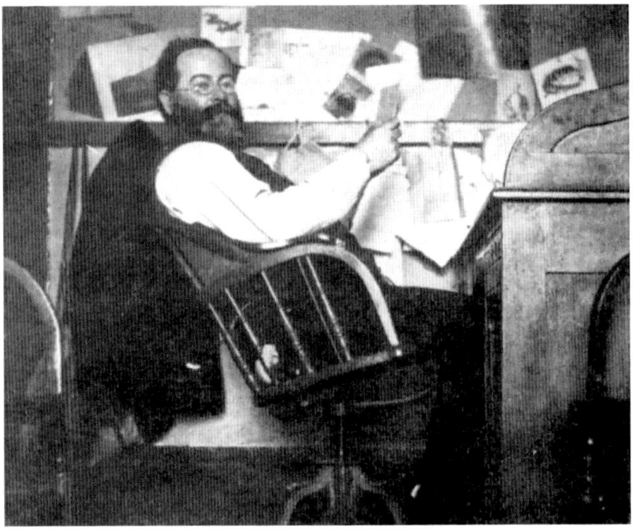

Scipio Craig, editor of the *Citrograph*, the newspaper created to promote Redlands, was unabashedly proud of his new city. With his bushy red beard and enthusiastic writing style, Craig named, and then steered, the newspaper its entire publishing life, from 1887 to his untimely death in 1908.

his pocket, just in case he ran into one of the culprits. Even though crime was not as rampant as now, more than once he nearly missed receiving a bullet aimed for someone else. L.E. Nelson, Redlands historian, wrote, "Trusted implicitly by both Anglos and Mexicans, Rivera smoothed adjustment amazingly as the latter became orange pickers in the valley, and he encouraged many to seek education and professional careers. His own son became a highly successful commercial artist in New York City, returning to Redlands at retirement."

In 1887, a group of local businessmen formed the Redlands News Company for the purpose of promoting the unification of Redlands and Lugonia. The men hired Scipio Craig as editor, and he became a passionate advocate for all things Redlands. Craig coined the name for the paper, the *Citrograph*, and his flamboyant style reflected the enthusiasm of early developers. When Lugonia was brought under the Redlands umbrella a year later, he rejoiced with abandon: "There is nothing too good for Redlands, the phenomenal city of wonderful California!"

It is said that Craig reported what he wanted and left out what he wanted. When a crime occurred, Craig was quick to report that the perpetrators came from San Bernardino. Craig would never acknowledge bad weather. If it was hot, "Blankets are at a slight discount for a few evenings past; there is a slight increase in the demand for fans." Of a sandstorm: "[It] had the effect of importing considerable Yuma real estate into our valley as well as to create activity in local dirt. The wind blew so hard at Colton and San Bernardino that both the Baptist and Methodist preachers who had exchanged pulpits with our local men failed to appear. There was no wind at the time in Redlands."

Craig was a man of many talents and interests. His physician father had trained him in medicine, and it was said that he "could set a leg or write a prescription; he was an authority on ores and mining, irrigation and forestry, and he could drive a locomotive."

The *Citrograph* and Scipio Craig never wavered in loyalty to Redlands. He called it "the scenic, productive, and climatic garden of the southland." With his red hair and beard, he was known to be friendly to all. Edith Parker Hinckley wrote, "He contributed untold benefits toward the growth and prosperity of Redlands by the high quality of his paper and by his enduring interest in its citizens."

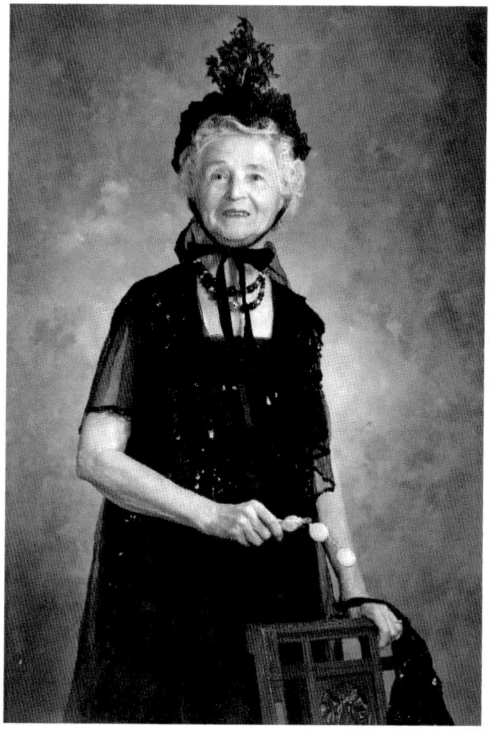

Edith and George Hinckley came to Redlands in 1908. George was hired to be the city's first engineer, and Edith soon immersed herself in civic affairs. In 1951, she published *On the Banks of the Zanja*, a definitive history of Redlands, much of which she had witnessed firsthand. Here she is dressed in historic costume in honor of Redlands' Diamond Jubilee in 1963.

Edith Parker and George Stevens Hinckley met as students at Pomona College. They married after their graduation in 1903 and came to Redlands in 1908. George Hinckley had been given the job of city engineer, and he oversaw the layout and development of the basic water and sewer services of the city. He was part of the boom years that produced our main roads and early tracts of housing.

Edith Hinckley grew to love her adopted town and turned her considerable writing talents to the preservation of its history. In 1951, she published her definitive work, *On the Banks of the Zanja: The Story of Redlands*. This was updated in a smaller volume in 1960 and also annotated to a school version called *Redlands Yesterdays*.

Mrs. Hinckley wrote histories of the Contemporary Club and the First Congregational Church, a biography of her father-in-law, Frank Hinckley, and two books of verse. She also collaborated on a history of Pomona College. Here was a woman who had enjoyed careers as a full-time mom, community volunteer, author and historian. You would think that would be enough for one lifetime, but in 1965, Hinckley returned to school. She earned a master's degree in English at the University of Redlands and wrote her thesis on "Crime and Scandal in Early Redlands." She was a mere eighty-four years old.

Hinckley went on to publish *Redlands and Certain Old-Timers* at the age of ninety. In 1984, the Moore Foundation published *Two Girls and a Kite, or Adventures Around the Kite-Shaped Track*, a manuscript penned by Hinckley and illustrated by her friend Ethel Burt after their graduation from Pasadena High School.

Larry Burgess, director of Smiley Library, provided annotations and wrote a biographical sketch of Hinckley in which he wrote, "Until the last months of her life when her fragile health restricted her activities, Edith Hinckley still read books from the library, reminisced with friends and family, and urged others to appreciate the history of their area. She died in her 101st year in July 1981."

The woman who brought Redlands history to life became part of the history in the process.

CLOTHESPINS, FLYTRAPS AND ROCKET FUEL—ALL INVENTED BY REDLANDERS

In my opinion, all previous advances in the various lines of invention will appear totally insignificant when compared with those which the present century will witness. I almost wish that I might live my life over again to see the wonders which are at the threshold.

–Charles H. Duell, U.S. commissioner of patents, 1899

The early Twentieth Century Redlanders seemingly consisted of two classes—those who had invented (or whose relatives had invented) some wealth-producing thing, enabling them to come to Redlands, or those in Redlands busily inventing things.

–Lawrence E. Nelson, Only One Redlands

At least two of Redlands' beautiful, century-old mansions were built by inventors. E.C. Sterling held the patents that controlled all the pressed bricks made in the United States. After his company became one of the country's largest commercial enterprises, he built his stately house above Crescent Avenue.

Getrude and Oliver Hicks came to Redlands and built All View on Knoll Road with the fortune they made from their patents. He patented and manufactured corrugated paper. She patented metal shoelace tips and a clip-on clothespin, as well as the paper bucket Americans still use to take home Chinese food and goldfish. Conveniently, Mr. Hicks's paper plant manufactured those containers, as well.

Early in the 1900s, the booming orange industry spawned a multitude of patents related to the packing and shipping of citrus and citrus byproducts. Homer Kingsbury invented a machine to squeeze lemons and a process that allowed lemon juice to keep indefinitely.

Henry Ruggles invented a variety of labor-saving machinery for packinghouses. He also invented pulp board boxes, and "four hundred visitors a day crowded to see oranges wrapped by machinery and packed in a hitherto waste product box."

A bubonic plague outbreak in 1909 inspired inventors to turn their creative impulses to the eradication of disease-carrying flies. First, W.A. McMillan got them out of your house with his "Turn-Around-and-Go-Out-Again" door and window screen:

> *The principle is a simple one, it being that a fly will not crawl downward behind a screen or bar, and consists of one screen overlapping another about a foot, the inner lap projecting away from the outer at the lower edge, so as to admit of easy access by flies walking up the inside of the screen. Arriving at the top edge of the outer screen the fly finds itself outside, and takes wing for other parts.*

Unfortunately, the fly flew away to infest again. A.E. Chapman came to the rescue with a trap utilizing the same principal but in reverse. His traps were placed at intervals along the street. Bait lured the flies into a wire cage; light from above drew them to walk upward and into the trap.

Chapman was hired as official fly catcher, with an office in city hall. Nelson continued:

> *Whew—3,700,000 flies caught…In twenty-five days he has emptied the traps of more than fifty gallons of flies. Inquiries from everywhere converged upon Redlands; who was Chapman and what was his secret? Mr. Chapman is considerable of a genius…He was the first man to perfect a vacuum*

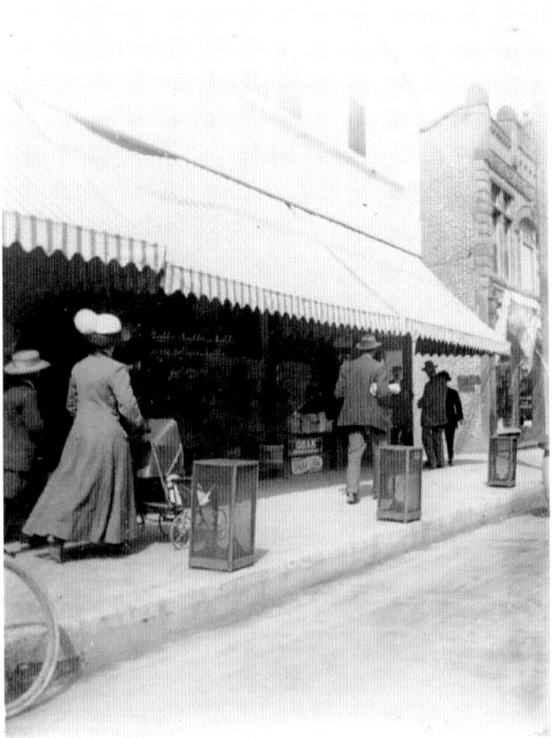

Flies were a real problem in the days before electricity-powered fans kept them at bay. In about 1910, this photograph of State Street shows a woman pushing her baby carriage past A.E. Chapman's flytraps. Millions of flies were trapped and recycled via a fish hatchery in Forest Home.

cleaner. He sold his rights to a firm in Pittsburgh. And now he had patented a folding fly trap, which could be shipped economically by freight anywhere.

In twelve months he personally captured 362 gallons of flies—21,000,000—in Redlands. Since he worked only the downtown area, and there were from 300 to 400 traps scattered through the residential section, there must have been in the neighborhood of 42,000,000 flies killed during the year... What became of the dead flies? The fish hatchery at Forest Home bought them, germs and all.

As the orange industry waned and the military moved into Norton Air Force Base, the patents from Redlanders shifted to related industries. Thus we find rocket fuels and propulsion technology in the late 1970s to mid-1980s. Medical technology leads the inventions of the most recent decades as Redlands researchers affiliated with Loma Linda Medical Center patent their medical advances, especially those associated with proton-beam therapy.

Meanwhile, I wonder where I could get one of Chapman's flytraps... summer's coming.

HINCKLEY'S WHITE LINE PAVED THE WAY

One of the historical "firsts" attributed to Redlands comes from a solution attributed to George Hinckley. Five years after his graduation from Pomona College in 1903, George Hinckley was hired to be Redlands' city engineer. Though he was initially disdained as "just a boy" in many eyes, Hinckley passed the test of time and served the town for thirty-eight years.

An early problem was the curve in the road at Cajon and Vine, the place where Cajon becomes Orange, where the grid of streets from the hills of Redlands (angled to take advantage of the slope for drainage) meets the north–south grid of the older town of Lugonia. As long as traffic was predominately horse and buggy, the curve posed no problem. Once the automobile was introduced in 1899, however, the road configuration took on new meaning. The new horseless vehicles were not equipped with our modern suspensions, and many overturned with little provocation.

Edith Parker Hinckley (George's wife) wrote of the solution in *On the Banks of the Zanja*: "After an automobile accident had occurred at the intersection of Vine and Cajon, Dr. M.W. Hill, who had an office in the Field Building on that corner [later the site of the Fox Theater building], came to the city engineer's office and said that something should be done to make that corner less of a hazard."

Popular Mechanics magazine in August 1911 reported the results:

> *A broad line of aluminum paint runs down the center of a western city street at a point where a sharp curve to the right is followed by an equally abrupt swerve to the left leading to a railroad crossing. The temptation is for drivers of autos to leave their own side of the street to shorten the corners. To prevent accidents, the novel plan was adopted of painting a central line and a guiding arrow. As the street is smoothly paved with asphalt, the bright white mark is very conspicuous. The innovation is the idea of George S. Hinckley, city engineer of Redlands, California.*

Edith Hinckley told us that an attorney advised her husband to patent his idea, but George declined, saying that it was a safety device and belonged to the public.

Hinckley oversaw the layout and development of the basic water and sewer services of the city. He was part of the first boom years that produced our main roads and early tracts of housing. By 1943, Hinckley must have been contemplating retirement, but one more serious problem roared down the local byways. Frank E. Moore, in his interesting and informative book *Redlands Astride the Freeway: The Development of Good Automobile Roads*, told of Hinckley's brainstorm to keep trucks from crashing into Redlands High School.

Tiny little Roosevelt Road carried all the Highway 99 traffic coming down the hill from Yucaipa into downtown Redlands. The highway doglegged left on Fern and then right a block later. A bypass was built so that traffic could curve more gently around the high school, but runaway trucks had trouble making the turn.

On February 27, 1943, the driver of a truck died after he lost control of his rig coming down the grade. Fortunately, it was a Saturday. The huge truck, loaded with lettuce and carrots, plowed straight through the high school grounds halfway to Citrus Avenue before it overturned.

Moore wrote:

> *Redlanders suddenly woke up. They wanted prompt insurance against a worse disaster.*
>
> *City engineer George Hinckley had a brainstorm. He would build a pond just downgrade from the entrance to the bypass. Runaway juggernauts would plunge straight into it. Hydraulic resistance would stop the truck. The driver would live.*

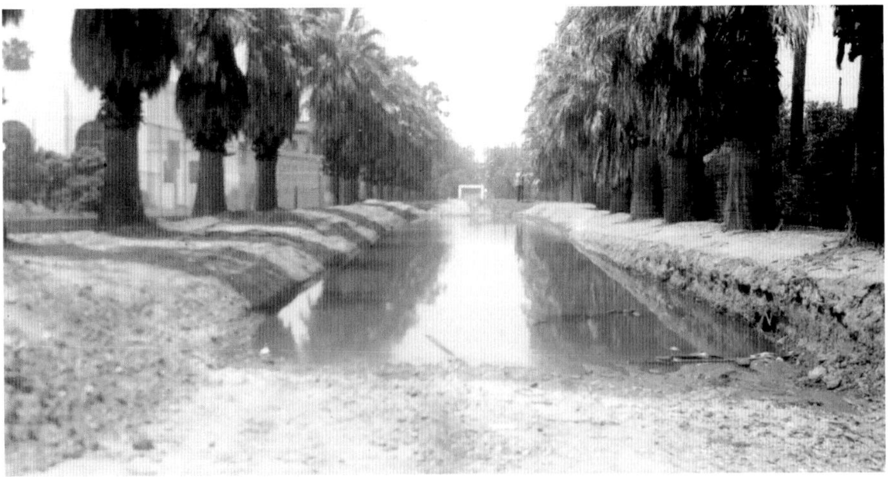

Before Highway 99 was constructed, the road from Yucaipa came down narrow Roosevelt Road. There was a sharp bend to take the roadway around Redlands High School. After a fatal accident in 1943, city engineer George Hinckley constructed a runaway truck pond to keep students safer on campus. On the left, you can see the wall of the original Terrier Gymnasium. The pond was never tested, as truck drivers preferred the risk of turning over onto the athletic fields to the chance of drowning.

> *There was no foolishness about environmental impact studies in those days. He didn't wait for anybody or anything. He just dispatched a crew with earth digging machines to the site. They tore up the pavement and bulldozed the dirt into embankments across the path on either side. The upper end was open for the runaways.*
>
> *How would it work? We'll never know. Truckers were more afraid of drowning than of trying to make the curve onto the bypass. As they swerved, their rigs would tip over spilling their loads on the edge of the girl's athletic playing field. Three years later the state built a four-lane highway* [now known as Redlands Boulevard] *a block to the west. Hinckley's truck trap was no longer needed.*

I wonder what unforeseen travel challenges will require a George Hinckley in our century?

Lighting Up the Streets of Redlands Was No Easy Task

In another "first," Redlands made the history books on September 7, 1893, when a switch was thrown, the crowd cheered and the band played with gusto as four electric arc lights illuminated the main intersection of town. The steady glow held back the night as our town proudly brought into existence electric streetlights powered by a first-in-the-world technology.

Henry Harbison Sinclair came to Redlands in 1887 for his health (most likely to overcome tuberculosis). A hydroelectrical engineer by training, he had been in the shipping business in New York. As he rested, "taking the cure" in Redlands, he became intrigued by the potential power source to be found from Mill Creek.

It was the dawn of the electrical age. Electric arc lamps had been installed in downtown Visalia and Santa Barbara. An electric company in Claremont was building a two-phase, alternating current generator, but no one had as yet solved the problem of how to deliver commercially usable electricity over a long distance from the source of its generation.

At the ripe young age of thirty-two, Sinclair organized the Redlands Electric Light and Power Company along with George H. Crafts, George B. Ellis and F.G. Feraud. They were granted a franchise by the city in 1892 and began making plans to build Mill Creek Power House No. 1 at a spot near the intake for the Zanja.

Sinclair enlisted the services of another young man, engineer Almarian W. Decker, and together they developed an electrical generating system radically different from any in use in the world at the time. Decker, also sick with tuberculosis, had tried to get someone to build a three-phase generator for the Claremont project, but the technology to do so was not invented yet. His partnership with the Redlands group happened to coincide with the birth of the General Electric Company, and the polyphase generators for the Mill Creek Plant No. 1 were its first big breakthrough.

In his 2007 Fortnightly Club paper, "Redlands Powers the World: How the San Bernardino Valley Developed Modern Electric Power First," Ronald Burgess wrote, "Decker's power generation and delivery system was so successful that it became the Southern California standard. The basic engineering was copied and built upon once again by Sinclair in the construction of the Santa Ana No. 1 plant, which in-turn was the model for more large projects, which in turn set the standard for the entire west."

Once Sinclair and Decker had their plans, the company set out to find financial backing. In her book *California Yankee*, Carol Green Wilson told of the financial difficulties encountered:

> *The Redlands Company had scraped together $10,000 as capital, but this was pitifully inadequate. Eastern investors were skittish about California schemes—too many scars remained from land-boom defaults. Money was tight. This was in 1893, year of the Great Panic. Sinclair returned to the Coast, and after strenuous campaigning in Los Angeles and then San Francisco, finally gave up and wired back to his colleagues, "Cannot place bonds, must abandon proposition." But a slow letter had been trailing along from Pittsburgh, to which the Fisher family had returned. Unaware of any hurry on the part of his former associates, Fisher had written, instead of wiring, his favorable answer to their appeal. Receiving this good news on the very day that Sinclair's discouraged message came down from San Francisco, Fulton G. Feraud, the Secretary of the Redlands Company, jovially wired back, "Come home, you dammed fool, Fisher takes the bonds."*

The Redlands Electric Company produced the first three-phase generators, the first synchronous motor and the first induction motor ever turned out for commercial use by the General Electric Company. With the backing of Henry Fisher, an oil millionaire who had recently moved to Redlands, Sinclair went on to organize the much larger Southern California Power Company, with the goal of sending electricity all the way to Los Angeles.

Ordinary People Made Extraordinary Contributions to Redlands History

In 1903, George P. Low wrote in *The Journal of Electricity Power and Gas*:

> *The great artery of the transmission system…is the main transmission line…which runs from the Santa Ana Canyon station almost in a direct line to…substation No. 1 in the city of Los Angeles. This is the far-famed 33,000-volt eighty-two-mile line, which for years was unequaled, both in length and voltage, by any line in the world. When the building of this line was projected under the voltages named, the project was strongly opposed by electrical manufacturing companies, who extended no encouragement whatever towards aiding the enterprise, and, in fact, the scheme met with very little encouragement of any character until after it had demonstrated its success.*

Sinclair and Fisher then joined with John B. Miller of Los Angeles to form the Edison Electric Company, now the Southern California Edison Company. Sinclair moved on to Pasadena, where he continued to be active in civic affairs.

Burgess continued:

> *Sadly, a victorious story turned bitter sweet for the brilliant Almarian Decker. Decker who single handedly designed the first complete system and*

History of Redlands, Mill Creek, Santa Ana Canyon, and various other early power lines of Edison Electric Company

[Trade Journal]

The Journal of Electricity, Power and Gas

San Francisco, CA, United States, January 1903

vol. XIII, no. 1, p. 9-24; 24-38; 42-46, col. 1-2

The Generating, Transmission and Distribution Systems of The Edison Electric Company of Los Angeles, Cal.

By Geo. P. Low

[Of all the world, America is infinitely far in the lead in the practical applications of transmission engineering, and of all America, California shows greater development along this line than any other State and the Union, yet to nowhere in California is there to be found more interesting long distance high voltage work of almost every conceivable description than exists in the southern portion of the State, where in a single system of The Edison Electric Company, of Los Angeles, alone may be marked not only the first polyphase transmission station ever built for commercial service in America, but where also may be traced, step-by-step, every advance made in the art of electric power transmission down to the present time. And the first among the prominent transmissions of southern California is this selfsame The Edison Electric Company, they principle hydraulic, mechanical and electrical features of which it is the purpose of this article to describe.

The Edison Electric Company of Los Angeles grew from the Redlands Electric Company. H.H. Sinclair and A.W. Decker, engineers for the Mill Creek Power Station No. 1, designed the first successful long-distance transmission of electricity fit for commercial use. This is an excerpt from the 1903 *Journal of Electricity Power and Gas* that goes on to describe Redlands' role in the dawn of the age of electricity.

probably created the demand for three-phase equipment development in the US, did not live to see his dream. His tuberculosis worsened in the summer of 1893, he was carried on a stretcher to view progress on other projects, but he never saw Mill Creek No 1 completed. The first commercially viable three-phase power plant in the world was running on September 7th 1893.

Back in Redlands, electricity was changing life in many ways. Though the arc lamps had to be cleaned every day, their illuminating properties were a wonder to all. Fisher extended his electrical investment to streetcars, replacing the mule-driven local ones and offering service to San Bernardino and surrounding areas. The Union Ice Company built a large plant in Mentone, and its cool products became available to homes and businesses.

L.E. Nelson noted that "Thaxter, the druggist, has put in a big electric fan, which makes the atmosphere very pleasant and shoos the flies all away from the soda fountain besides. This latter is a real luxury."

The life of H.H. Sinclair is a lesson in perseverance. He overcame a serious illness, financial hardship (at one time he had a forty-dollar mortgage on his cow) and doubting "experts" to see his dreams come true. As I sit in my air-conditioned office, writing on my computer, I am quite thankful that he did.

HIGH SCHOOL GRADUATION TRADITIONS GO BACK TO THE EARLY YEARS

All the tickets for the High School commencement are given out, and there are still numerous applicants.

–Redlands Daily Facts, *June 1894*

Redlands Unified School District high school graduation traditions can trace their roots back to the first high school in the city. Twelve students formed the first graduating class of Redlands High School in June 1894. The ceremony was held in the Academy of Music building (northeast corner of Citrus and Orange). From 1905 to 1916, the ceremonies were held at the Wyatt Opera House (northwest corner of Colton and Orange). In 1917, the commencement exercises were moved to the Municipal Amphitheater, later to become the Redlands Bowl, in Smiley Park.

A group of top-ranked junior class girls and boys help honor the seniors, a tradition going back to the Daisy Chain at Redlands High School. No mention of the Daisy Chain appears in the *Makio* (founded in 1906, the

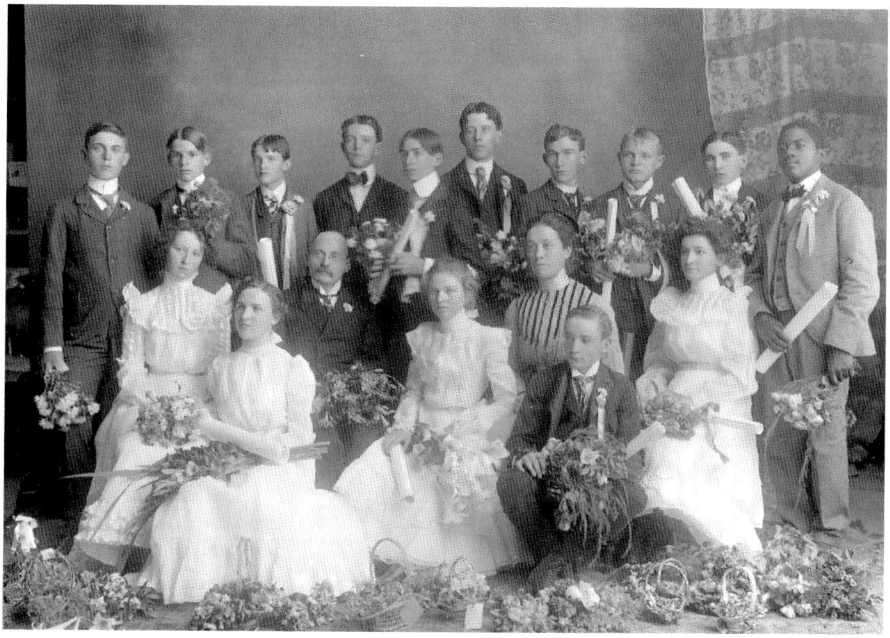

A Redlands High School class circa 1900 poses with their diplomas. Bedecked with flowers, with girls in white dresses and boys in formal suits, the early years established many of the traditions that continue in the graduation ceremonies of today's three comprehensive high schools in the Redlands Unified School District.

oldest yearbook in the state) until 1933, but Class Night programs and newspaper reports show this to be a very long-lived tradition. The early Daisy Chain members were chosen by senior girls as a sort of popularity contest. The procedure was formalized in 1933. A committee of eleven senior girls was chosen to make the selection of thirty junior girls from a pool of fifty nominees. The report in that year's *Makio* goes on to say that "[t]he girls were judged by their ability to refrain from passing on gossip; by the way in which they handled a job given them to do; by their scholastic standing; by their popularity and modesty; and by all other qualities which are necessary to every true type of girlhood."

This selection process evolved into one of academic standing. Today, the top students of the Redlands High School junior class are honored to be Daisy Chain (girls) or Junior Ushers (boys). At Redlands East Valley, the group is called the Honor Court. Citrus Valley recognized the first members of its junior class honor group, the Discipuli Dignitatis, in 2012.

Until the mid-1950s, students wore formals and dark suits as graduation attire. The class of 1955 was the first to vote to wear caps and gowns—for

Baccalaureate only. As long as it could hold them, graduating students sat on the stage facing the audience of parents and friends. It must have been lovely: girls in white dresses holding colorful flowers and boys with starched shirts and suits.

Lois Fair Wilson shared a folder of graduation and reunion mementos kept over the years by her late mother, Emma Lederer Fair, Redlands High School class of 1913. There were seventy-three members of the class of 1913. They were said to be a "livewire group." They graduated at the Wyatt Opera House instead of the not-yet-built Redlands Bowl, but otherwise many of their traditions were the same as now. Junior girls with chains of ivy and daisies escorted the seniors, the stage was decorated with flowers and the year "1913" was formed in flowers and hung from the backdrop. Bearing diplomas signed by Fred H. Clock and H.G. Clement, names familiar as school buildings to current Redlands students, the Redlands High School class of 1913 graduated unaware that the world was on the brink of World War I.

The 1913 *Daily Facts* included a list of students and their post-graduation plans. Emma Lederer (as well several others, men and women) declared her intention to seek employment as a stenographer. Lederer went to work for the *Daily Facts*; in 1918, when the United States threw its full support behind the Allies in Europe, she became a "government girl," working in Washington, D.C., until 1919, when the end of World War I saw a legion of women discharged from "war work" and sent back to their hometowns.

No mention of an alma mater appears until 1942, when the program opened with "Pomp and Circumstance" and closed with the playing of "The Alma Mater" on the carillon of the Methodist church. When the Methodist church burned down in late June 1967, the carillon given to that church in 1923 by the Watchorn family was lost. Graduates of the next few years remember the alma mater being played by orchestra chimes on the stage of the bowl.

Fortunately, Wilbur Showalter, longtime head of the RHS Music Department, spearheaded the donation and purchase of a new carillon. Called the Shirk Coronation Carillon (arranged as a surprise honor to Mary Kimberly Shirk), it was housed in the First Congregational Church. Like the Watchorn Chimes, a carillon player in the church could be signaled from the Prosellis at the end of the singing of the alma mater.

Today, the tradition continues with the Ray Mills Carillon installed at the First Congregational Church in 2010. The Shirk Carillon had fallen into disrepair, and Ed Huston, looking for an honor for his friend, the late Ray Mills, thought that a new carillon would give back to the community in a way befitting the former Redlands Man of the Year. A Redlands native,

Mills had served Redlands Fire Department for thirty-two years and was fire chief from 1980 to 1991.

Today's graduates of the three Redlands high schools and their families still enjoy the beautiful setting of the Redlands Bowl. For three nights in a row in June, students are admonished to dress nicely and not chew gum. Noisemakers, beach balls and balloons are not allowed. The ceremony is happy yet dignified, a fine tribute to tradition. Escorted by their junior class honor students, the graduates file into the bowl, wearing caps and gowns in variations of their school colors. They all march to the tune of "Pomp and Circumstance." Speeches are made, talented musicians showcase their abilities and the diplomas are presented.

It has been important for each school to establish its own traditions. Bagpipes play the alma mater and fireworks end the ceremonies for Redlands East Valley. The Citrus Valley High School ceremony closes to the voices of the choir, Lumier du Chanson, singing the Citrus Valley alma mater.

As for Redlands High School, after the clapping subsides, all stand to sing their school's alma mater. The words fade away, everyone quiet, as the carillon takes up the tune one last time to end the ceremonies. The beauty of the setting and the closing ceremonies make for an emotional moment for all to remember forever.

Redlands Teacher Began Custom of Pledging to the Flag

Among the many "firsts" attributed to Redlands is the distinction given to Kingsbury School by its famous first-grade teacher, Miss Mary Fackler. Fackler began the tradition of schoolchildren giving a daily salute to the United States' flag.

The Pledge of Allegiance, written by Francis Bellamy in honor of the 400th anniversary of Columbus's discovery of America, was used in Redlands' 1892 Columbus Day program. After the ceremonies, the Pledge was forgotten by everyone except Fackler. Edith Parker Hinckley, in *Redlands and Certain Old-Timers*, quoted her: "We had the salute only at the end of a day…A child who had not been tardy or absent, and who had been especially good in his lessons on that day, was allowed to hold the standard while the others saluted it."

A certain General Breckenridge, visiting from Washington, D.C., heard of Fackler's new tradition and was so impressed by the sight of the children and their patriotism that he arranged to have the Pledge of Allegiance given in

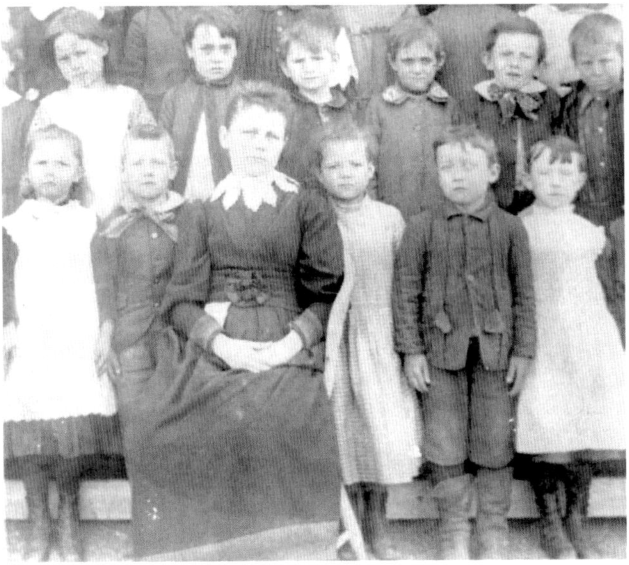

Mary Fackler, the first first-grade teacher for Kingsbury School, poses with her class. Smiles were impossible as subjects were required to hold their poses without movement long enough for the film to be exposed.

front of a large gathering when he returned to the Capitol. His wife wrote to Fackler, "All the distinguished men and women in the East were there and the children gave the salute, which was beautiful and impressive and created… much applause. It was mentioned as coming from the California children. I thought that you would like to know it, since it is all owing to you."

It was my pleasure to know two of Fackler's former students. Olive and Emma Jane Lawson were both born in Redlands and lived here all their lives. The Lawsons shared some of their personal memories of Miss Fackler and Kingsbury School.

Financed by the *unanimous* passage of two $15,000 bonds, Kingsbury was opened in 1888 and was added to in 1891. It was a magnificent building. Like many early structures in Redlands, the school was two stories, made of brick and anchored with a large bell tower. The Lawsons said that they might have been about the last ones to remember Mr. Cotter, the janitor, who rang the bell. In his blue- and white-striped bib overalls, Cotter would stand at the base of the tower and pull on the long rope that ran up to the bell itself. The tower was forbidden territory, but certain groups of boys were known to sneak in and climb to the top to chase after the owls that nested there.

Questions of earthquake safety coupled with the inevitable overcrowding that still plagues us today led to the demolition of the "old" Kingsbury building and its reincarnation twice again to its present state as one of the larger elementary schools. Those with children in today's crowded schools

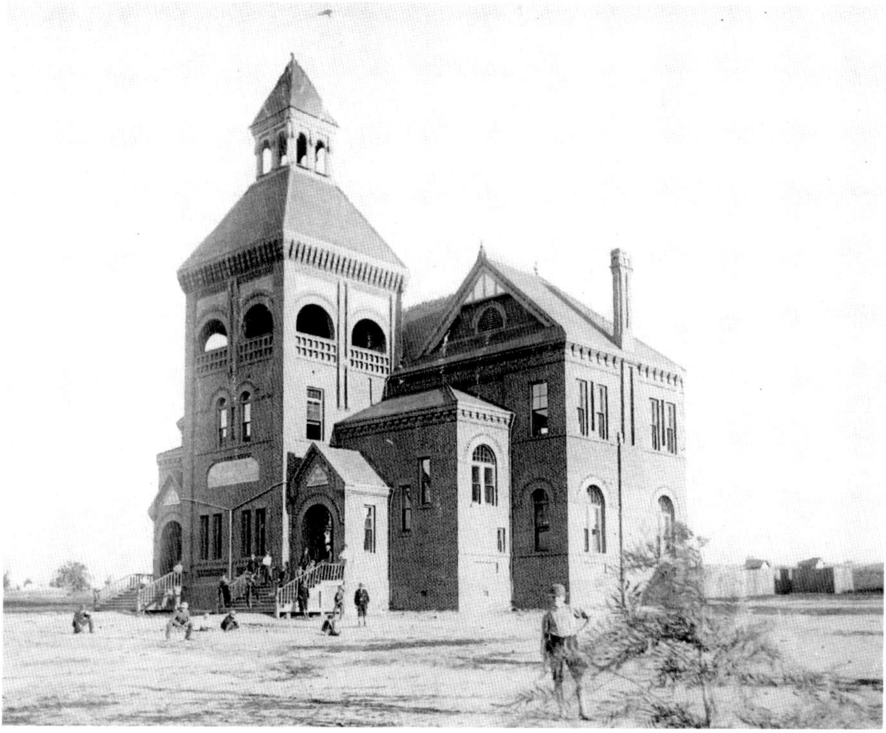

The original Kingsbury School, on the southwest corner of Cypress and Cajon, had four classrooms, two on either side of the central tower. A close look beyond the right corner of the building probably shows the student outhouses.

might find it interesting to know that when Kingsbury was opened in 1888 with four rooms, Miss Fackler had sixty-eight pupils but seats for only fifty-six, Miss Paine had sixty-four pupils and seats for fifty-five and Miss Hurley had seventy pupils and seats for fifty-five. Those numbers make our current thirty-five to thirty-seven students per classroom sound luxurious.

Fackler retired in 1921 but continued to offer private tutoring in her home. The Lawson sisters also remember her well in this role. Fackler lived in a pretty cottage at 232 Cajon Street (now a commercial building). Her piano teaching sister lived nearby. The Lawson girls would take the streetcar from their home on Chestnut Street down the hill to piano lessons and tutoring from the Fackler sisters. The girls wore a book of tickets on a string around their necks, and the driver would pull one off for each ride.

Fackler was known to be very handy with both a needle and a hammer. She tackled remodeling jobs herself, once building a partition in her home to divide one large room into two. One day, she lost a hammer into the wall space below a window she was repairing. It dropped too far for her to retrieve, so she wrote a poem explaining how, as it was a fair day, she had been working with the windows open. She folded the poem into a bottle and dropped it down to join the hammer.

Another time, Fackler boarded up a closet with a bookshelf and realized too late that she would not be able to remove a trunk that lived in the closet. She again wrote a poem and put it into the trunk for someone to find at a later date.

Miss Mary Fackler's maxim for her first graders was "Teach them to read," but I wouldn't be surprised to hear that she'd joined the boys at the top of the bell tower.

THE FIGHT FOR PROSPECT PARK WAS WON THE REDLANDS WAY

Historic Prospect Park, original home to the Redlands Colony and later a lushly landscaped park of orange groves and roadways designed to showcase the spectacular views, had been open to the public since its inception in the late 1800s. Along with Cañon Crest, the larger marvel of the Smiley brothers on a hill to the west, it was a major tourist attraction in the early part of the 1900s. Presidents William McKinley and Theodore Roosevelt had both taken the horse-drawn carriage tour of these parks during their visits to Redlands.

Many orange groves gave way to houses in the late 1950s and early 1960s, and the city let Cañon Crest go to subdivision. When it seemed that Prospect Park would be subdivided as well, community members went into action and organized a bond proposal to save the park.

The Prospect Park bond election of October 1963 failed to pass, but the Prospect Park Committee took the disappointing news in stride. The very next day, a group of sixty-seven stalwart supporters met to plan a new strategy. They recognized that Redlanders did not want to go into debt to purchase the park but believed that there was enough backing in the community to raise the money outright.

An escrow was opened at the Bank of America Redlands branch on November 5, 1963, for the purpose of collecting contributions. Those who donated were promised the return of their funds if the goal was not reached by December 1. This optimistic start was first extended to April 1964 and would eventually become one of the longest escrows in bank history. Early and later donors graciously allowed their money to remain on hold in the hopes that the park property would eventually be acquired.

The total amount needed was $560,000. By the end of April 1964, about $137,000 had been pledged or donated. As 1964 slipped into 1965 and 1966, the U.S. Congress passed the Housing and Urban Development Act, which allowed Redlands to apply for 50 percent of the needed funds from this federal source.

In 1967, Dr. Edmund Dombrowski agreed to be permanent chairman of the Prospect Park Committee. His commitment rejuvenated the effort, and the fundraising began anew. The committee's plan was to involve as many citizens as possible. Between June 1967 and January 1968, more than ten major fundraising activities were held: a Baja fishing trip, two auctions, a small circus featuring Buffo the Clown, the Ice Follies, a garden tour and numerous Prospect Park open houses.

This veritable mountain of effort involved the entire community. Hundreds of names are listed as chairmen of committees, organizers of phone trees, decorations, reservations and more. Alas, the goodwill was much greater than the dollars raised, and a deadline from HUD of February 6, 1968, was looming.

In his article in *The Prospect Park Book*, Julian Blakeley chronicled the saga of "The Winning of Prospect Park." Space does not permit me to include most of the names of individuals who worked so hard on the project. It is a reminder of the breadth of public support in this community.

By January 1968, the Prospect Park Committee was $60,000 shy of its goal and must have been wondering if their dream would ever become a reality. Leon Armantrout organized ten teams for a make-or-break endeavor that resulted in the raising of $40,000 and a 120-day extension from HUD. The goal was tantalizingly close but still elusive.

The effort might have failed but for the stunning announcement made by Mary Kimberly Shirk on January 29, 1968. As a "stimulus" to the campaign to save Prospect Park, Mrs. Shirk was offering to donate her family home, Kimberly Crest, and its gardens to a private foundation for the use and enjoyment of the people of Redlands…but only if Prospect Park was saved.

The Kimberly family had owned their French chateau on the hill adjoining Prospect Park since 1906. Helen Kimberly and her daughter, Mary Kimberly Shirk, had become two of Redlands' best-known patronesses. Mrs. Shirk's ultimate gift to her beloved city was the gift of preservation. She said that she wanted Kimberly Crest to be preserved, a monument to her mother, as an example of the way people lived in the early part of the twentieth century.

Mrs. Shirk's public spirit proved contagious. The Prospect Park Committee approached the then-current property owners, Mrs. Fred Hill, David Hill and Ralph Sechrest, with the request that they consider

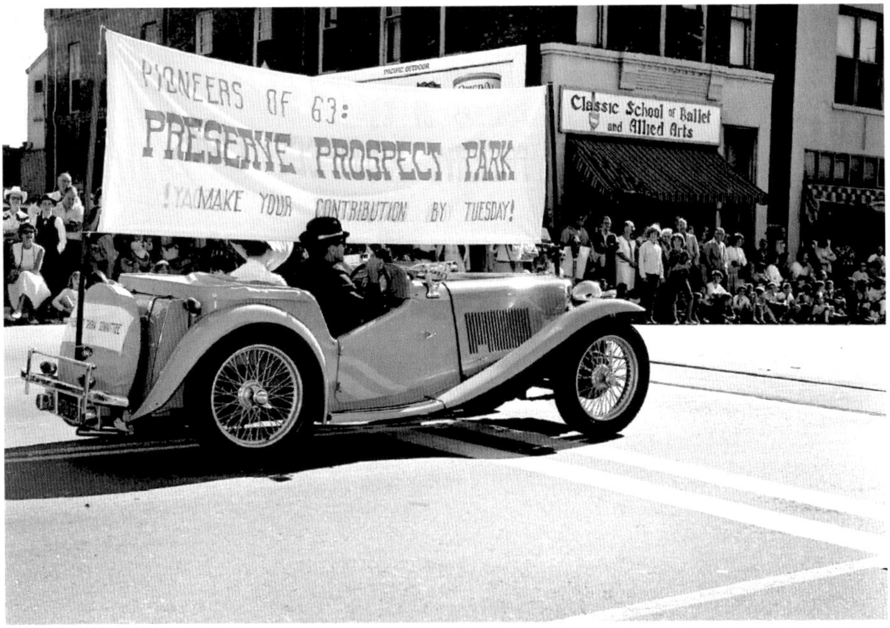

Margie and Leon Armantrout drive a vintage automobile down Orange Street as part of a fundraising parade for Prospect Park. Between 1963 and 1968, the citizens of Redlands struggled, and finally succeeded, to raise funds to match a federal grant that allowed them to hand Prospect Park to the city.

a lower purchase price for the property. After an overnight consultation with family members, they called back to say, "It's yours."

On August 9, 1968, a representative of HUD presented the city with a check matching the $212,019.37 donated by the citizens of Redlands. The escrow was finally closed.

Blakeley wrote, "This transfer of funds took place in Prospect Park on a gentle summer morning just like a thousand others—now just a little brighter because Prospect Park belonged to the citizens of Redlands."

Though it is part of the city park system, Prospect Park continues to be supported by a volunteer group, the Friends of Prospect Park. The Avis Meeker Sewall Theater in the park pays tribute to another generous Redlands benefactor. The carriage house, built by the England family in 1897, was completely restored in the 1990s and hosts small concerts, weddings and other parties. Middle school and high school cross-country teams showcase the park with their races, and countless joggers and dog walkers admire the paths and the views.

To quote Mayor Waldo Burroughs, this is "the Redlands way."

References

Bauer, Dale, and (Alma) Gene Bauer. "The Bauer Daffodil Garden—Did It Just Happen?" Fortnightly Club of Redlands, March 16, 2006. http://www.redlandsfortnightly.org/papers/Bauer06.html.

Beattie, George William, and Helen Pruitt Beattie. *Heritage of the Valley: San Bernardino's First Century*. Oakland, CA: Biobooks, 1951.

Bromberger, Frederick S. "The Nordhoff Trilogy." Fortnightly Club of Redlands, December 14, 1995.

Burgess, Larry E. "Forty Years Toiling in the Historical Vineyard." Fortnightly Club of Redlands, December 15, 2011. http://www.redlandsfortnightly.org/papers/burgess11.htm.

———. *The Smileys: A Commemorative Edition*. Redlands, CA: Moore Historical Foundation, 1991.

Burgess, Larry E., and Nathan D. Gonzales. *Faithfully and Liberally Sustained: Philanthropy in Redlands.* Redlands, CA: Esri Press, 2010.

———. *Redlands*. Charleston, SC: Arcadia, 2004.

Burgess, Ronald L. "Redlands Powers the World: How the San Bernardino Valley Developed Modern Electric Power First." Fortnightly Club of Redlands, California, January 18, 2007. http://www.redlandsfortnightly.org/papers/burgessRon07.htm.

Guideposts to History: People and Places of Historical Significance in Early San Bernardino and Riverside Counties. Santa Fe, CA: Santa Fe Federal Savings and Loan Association, 1977.

Hinckley, Edith Barrett Parker. *On the Banks of the Zanja: The Story of Redlands*. Claremont, CA: Saunders Press, 1951.

———. *Redlands and Certain Old-timers*. Claremont, CA: Creative Press, 1970.

Irshay, Phyllis C. *The Pride and Glory of the Town: The Story of the A.K. Smiley Public Library*. Redlands: City of Redlands, California, 1988.

Low, George P. *Journal of Electricity Power and Gas* 13 (January–December 1903). http://books.google.com/books?id=1qQvAAAAYAAJ&printsec=frontcover&dq=Journal+of+electricity+power+and+gas+1903&hl=en&sa=X&ei=zlWwT9i6KMiUiQLhyO3sAw&sqi=2&ved=0CDsQ6AEwAA#v=onepage&q=Journal%20of%20electricity%20power%20and%20gas%201903&f=false.

Milner, Clyde A., Carol A. O'Connor and Martha A. Sandweiss. *The Oxford History of the American West*. New York: Oxford University Press, 1994.

Moore, Frank E. *Redlands Astride the Freeway: The Development of Good Automobile Roads*. Redlands, CA: Moore Historical Foundation, 1995.

———. *Redlands, Our Town*. Redlands, CA: Moore Historical Foundation, 1987.

———. *With a Grain of Salt: A Collection of Columns*. Redlands, CA: Moore Historical Foundation, 1985.

Moore, William G. *Fun with Fritz: Adventures in Early Redlands, Big Bear, and Hollywood with John H. "Fritz" Fisher*. Redlands, CA: Moore Historical Foundation, 1986.

———. *Redlands Yesterdays: A Photo Album, 1870–1920*. Redlands, CA: Moore Historical Foundation, 1983.

Nelson, Lawrence Emerson. *Only One Redlands: Changing Patterns in a Southern California Town*. Redlands, CA: Community Music Association, 1963.

Robinson, John W. *The San Bernardinos: The Mountain Country from Cajon Pass to Oak Glen: Two Centuries of Changing Use*. Arcadia, CA: Big Santa Anita Historical Society, 1989.

Simpson, Lee M.A. *Selling the City: Gender, Class, and the California Growth Machine, 1880–1940*. Stanford, CA: Stanford University Press, 2004.

Sonnichsen, Charles L. *Col. Greene and the Copper Skyrocket*. Tucson: University of Arizona Press, 1974.

Wilson, Carol Green. *California Yankee: William R. Staats, Business Pioneer*. Claremont, CA: Saunders Press, 1946.

About the Author

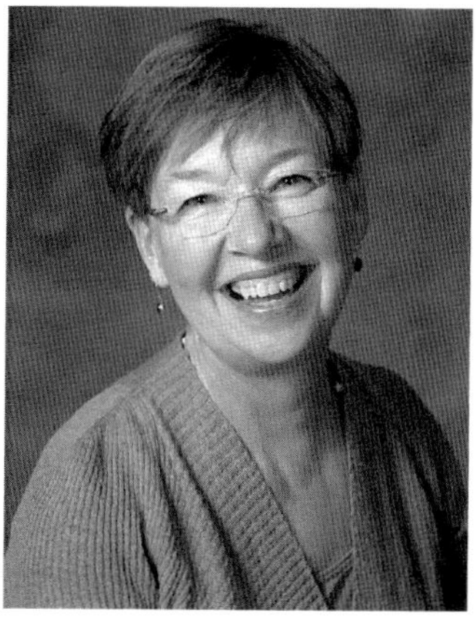

Joan Hedges McCall has been a well-known educator and community volunteer in Redlands, California, for more than thirty years. She has been a member of the Redlands Heritage Auxiliary, serving as scriptwriter, school tour chair and board member. Her monthly column, "Regarding Redlands," and numerous feature articles have appeared in the *Redlands Daily Facts*. Joan McCall has been a history teacher and a teacher librarian. She holds a BA degree from Pomona College and an MA degree from Azusa Pacific University.